EXPLORING THE CONTEXTS FOR EARLY LEARNING

The concept of 'readiness for school' is attractive to policy-makers, but many academics, researchers and practitioners argue that an early start to formal learning may be misguided. This book introduces readers to an increasing body of evidence which demonstrates that young children need opportunities to learn and develop in environments that support their emotional and cognitive needs, offering opportunities to develop autonomy, competence and self-regulation skills.

With advice on implementing research findings in practice, this book provides clear guidance on how to foster and develop these attributes, scaffold steps into new areas of learning and support children in facing new challenges. Chapters cover:

- Policy and discourses
- Taking account of development
- Approaches to early years learning
- The diversity of children's early experiences
- Transitions and starting school
- Where to in the future?

Exploring the Contexts for Early Learning will be essential reading for students, practitioners, policy-makers and all those interested in the school readiness agenda.

Rory McDowall Clark was formerly a Senior Lecturer in the Centre for Early Childhood at the University of Worcester, UK for many years. She taught across a range of programmes including BA, PGCE and MA degrees in Early Childhood Studies.

Research informed professional development for the early years

TACTYC (Association for Professional Development in Early Years)

Each book in this series focuses on a different aspect of research in early childhood which has direct implications for practice and policy. They consider the main research findings which should influence practitioner thinking and reflection and help them to question their own practice alongside activities to deepen knowledge and extend understanding of the issues. Readers will benefit from clear analysis, critique and interpretation of the key factors surrounding the research as well as examples and case studies to illustrate the research–practice or research–policy links. Supporting the development of critical reflection and up-to-date knowledge, the books will be a core resource for all those educating and training early years practitioners.

Exploring the Contexts for Early Learning
Challenging the school readiness agenda
Rory McDowall Clark

Forthcoming titles:

Places for 2 Year Olds in the Early Years
Supporting learning and development
Jan Georgeson and Verity Campbell-Barr

Young Children Are Researchers
Building knowledge in early childhood
Jane Murray

Supporting Abused and Neglected Children in the Early Years
Practice, policy and provision
Sue Soan

EXPLORING THE CONTEXTS FOR EARLY LEARNING

Challenging the school readiness agenda

Rory McDowall Clark

 Routledge
Taylor & Francis Group

LONDON AND NEW YORK

First published 2017
by Routledge
2 Park Square, Milton Park, Abingdon, Oxon OX14 4RN

and by Routledge
711 Third Avenue, New York, NY 10017

Routledge is an imprint of the Taylor & Francis Group, an informa business

British Library Cataloguing in Publication Data
A catalogue record for this book is available from the British Library

Library of Congress Cataloging in Publication Data
Names: Clark, Rory McDowall, author.
Title: Exploring the contexts for early learning : challenging
the school readiness agenda / Rory McDowall Clark.
Description: New York, NY : Routledge, 2016. | Includes
bibliographical references.
Identifiers: LCCN 2016017215 | ISBN 9781138937826 (hardback) |
ISBN 9781138937833 (pbk.) | ISBN 9781315676036 (ebook)
Subjects: LCSH: Readiness for school. | Early childhood education. |
Cognition in children. | Metacognition in children.
Classification: LCC LB1132 .C53 2016 | DDC 372.21—dc23LC
record available at https://lccn.loc.gov/2016017215

ISBN: 978-1-138-93782-6 (hbk)
ISBN: 978-1-138-93783-3 (pbk)
ISBN: 978-1-315-67603-6 (ebk)

Typeset in Bembo
by diacriTech, Chennai

CONTENTS

ACKNOWLEDGEMENTS

This book draws on a research report prepared for TACTYC by Sue Bingham and David Whitebread.

Thank you to Jan Georgeson, Nancy Stewart and, in particular, Janet Moyles, for helpful and supportive critical feedback on the text.

Thanks also to Rosie Slocombe for some new perspectives on old ideas.

SERIES EDITORS' PREFACE

Professor Emerita Janet Moyles and Professor Jane Payler

Welcome to the first volume in the new, inspiring TACTYC book series. As part of the Association for Professional Development in the Early Years, TACTYC members believe that effective early years policies and practices should be informed by an understanding of the findings and implications of high quality, robust research. TACTYC focuses on developing the knowledge base of all those concerned with early years education and care by creating, reviewing and disseminating research findings and by encouraging critical and constructive discussion to foster reflective attitudes in practitioners. Such a need has been evident in the resounding success of events such as our conferences where speakers make clear connections between research and practice for delegates. Early years practitioners and those who support their professional development engage enthusiastically with early childhood research and understand how it is likely to impact upon, and enhance, practice. They acknowledge that research has a distinct role to play in effective work in early years education and care, and that they should be part of a 'research-rich education system'.

TACTYC is an organisation with a specific focus on the professional development of all those involved in early childhood with the express purpose of improving practices to enhance the well-being of young children. Its reputation for quality research and writing includes its international *Early Years* journal. This book series is likely to be popular with those who value the journal as it will add to its range and scope. Our aim for the series is to help those who educate and train early years practitioners at all levels to understand the implications and practical interpretation of recent research, and to offer a rationale for improving the quality and reach of practice in early years education and care.

It is not always easy for busy trainers and practitioners to access contemporary research and translate it into informed and reflective practice. These books are intended to promote the benefits of applying research in an informed way to develop quality pedagogical practices. Each individual book in this series will explore a range of different topics within a theme. This first book considers the issues involved in *children's readiness for school*. It teases out the implications of research and theory and presents these in a clear, unambiguous way, while acknowledging the often complex relationships between what we know and what is possible in practice.

Interest in this phase of education and care has been growing exponentially in the last few years, and there is now a rich source of early years research on which writers may draw. The claim is frequently made that policies are 'evidence-based' but this is not the same as rigorous, impartial research. Many policy and practice documents purport to be based on 'evidence', but this depends to a large extent on the political framework and ideology in place at different periods in time – few governments have the scope in their relatively short elected periods to give strategic consideration to the complex implications of different research outcomes for policies and practice. What is politically and economically expedient at the time is too often the driving force behind decisions about young children and their families.

All the writers in this series have been asked to present their particular focus, and to outline the issues and challenges within that framework which are relevant for early years practitioners. Exploring aspects of early years practice, based on research and sound theoretical underpinning, the writers will offer guidance on how findings can be analysed and interpreted to inform the continuing process of developing high quality early years practice. They will examine the research background to each topic and offer considered views on why the situation is as it is, and how it might move forward within the frameworks of imposed curricula and assessments. They will offer thoughtful advice to practitioners for dealing with the challenges faced within that particular focus and will suggest relevant follow-up reading and web-based materials to support further reflection, practice and curriculum implementation. Each book will also identify where further research is needed and will help tutors, trainers and practitioners to understand how they can contribute to research in this field.

Early years education and care is universally contentious, especially in relation to how far those outside the field, e.g. politicians and policy-makers, should intervene in deciding what constitutes successful early years pedagogy, curriculum and assessment. The main focus of the series will be on practice, policy and provision in the UK, but writers will also draw on international research perspectives, as there is a great deal to learn from colleagues in other national contexts.

The series particularly targets readers qualified at Level 6, or students on such courses, preparing for roles in which they will be expected to educate and train other practitioners in effective early years practices. There will be many others who will find the books invaluable: leaders of early years settings, who often have an education, training and professional development role in relation to their staff (and may well be qualified at Level 6 or beyond) will similarly find the series useful in their work. Academics and new researchers who support the training and development of graduate leaders in early years will also appreciate the books in this series. Readers will benefit from clear analysis, critique and interpretation of the key factors surrounding the research as well as exemplifications and case studies to illustrate the links between research and policy as well as research and practice. The books will support the development of critical reflection and up-to-date knowledge, and will be a core resource for all those educating and training early years practitioners,

In summary, research-based early years practice is a relatively new field as much of practitioners' work with young children over recent years has been based on the implementation of policy documents, which are often not grounded in rigorous, clear, unambiguous research evidence. The main aim of the TACTYC series is to help tutors and trainers to enable practitioners to become more informed advocates for provision of high quality services for children and their families. This will be achieved by promoting the benefits of applying research in an informed way to develop the quality of practice.

INTRODUCTION

1958: A young girl stands in the playground holding her mother's hand as they wait in line for their turn to register for the Reception class at the local Primary School. The girl is coming up to her fifth birthday and excited about starting school. When they reach the front of the queue the headmistress writes down the child's name, address and date of birth and then her mother waves goodbye as another lady takes her inside to the classroom. The girl looks round with curiosity – there are so many interesting things to play with she doesn't know where to begin: should it be painting or plasticine? There are lots of picture books to look at or maybe she'll draw a picture with the crayons. A few children are crying; this puzzles her when there are so many exciting things to do, but she ignores them and goes over to the home corner where a couple of other children are already playing.

1984: It is mid-September and a young boy is starting school today. He is so excited that he woke up early and dressed himself in his new school uniform but he can't manage the tie on his own. To ease transition into school the children have a staggered start and will only attend for half the day over the first couple of weeks, so his mother reminds him he will have to wait until after lunch. As there are still several hours to go, Mum sidetracks him by teaching him how to fasten his tie. He is immensely proud of this achievement and tells his little brother that he'll be able to go to school when he is a big boy too. After lunch, all three walk to school together and Mum has a chance to talk to the teacher about her son's interests and past experience whilst he plays in the sand tray with the other child who started this afternoon.

Present day: It is the first day of term and thirty children arrive in the Reception class. For a considerable number the environment is not new as it is next to where they spent the previous 12 to 21 months in the Nursery, so they are familiar with the shared environment of the Foundation Stage outdoor play area. A couple of children are new to the school, but the teacher has laid foundations for a relationship through a home visit, settling sessions in the summer term and a meeting with the child's key worker from their previous setting, who was able to share information from their Learning Journey gathered since beginning their out-of-home education at 18 months old. There is little time for being worried as there is so much to do, but grown-ups are there to help each child say goodbye to Mum and Dad and guide them to their chosen activity.

Three generations of children starting school – many details have changed over this time, but much remains the same, notably young children themselves and their curiosity, playfulness and eagerness to learn. Most readers will remember their own experiences in Reception class – playing in the class shop or the water tray, painting and drawing, making models out of play-dough (or plasticine depending on your age), singing songs, reciting rhymes and gathering around the teacher's chair to listen to stories. At the time we were unaware that we were developing the foundations for numeracy, literacy and science whilst our teachers, who understood the value of these activities, had the opportunity to get to know each pupil's individual skills and the areas where they needed extra support and encouragement. The child in the first vignette above is me and the fact that the memory remains vivid so many years later testifies to the huge significance of the event in young children's lives; it is similarly momentous for parents as I recall from taking my own son to school for the first time nearly thirty years later.

Whilst new generations of young children continue to enter the school gates to embark on formal schooling, the political influences, ideological discourses and the macro policy context that affects what they will experience have changed out of all recognition. The point when education becomes formalised and children are required to conform to externally imposed outcomes is reached earlier as children now enter the Reception class at age four. Despite having 20 per cent less life experience and maturity than five-year-olds, however, expectations of them have progressively grown. This is a situation that increasingly worries educators, parents, academics and researchers; meanwhile children themselves have no say in the matter and simply accept the situations they encounter.

An extensive body of research recognises that early childhood education improves children's well-being, helps create a foundation for lifelong learning, makes learning outcomes more equitable, reduces the effects of poverty and has the potential to improve social mobility across generations. This has brought education for the youngest children into sharp focus; indeed increasing policy attention has become a worldwide trend as the burgeoning knowledge economy leads governments to invest more heavily in early years provision. As a result the notion of school readiness has been gaining attention as a strategy for economic development (UNICEF 2012).

Over recent years increasing reference to the notion of 'school readiness' in official discourse has sparked extensive discussion, but limited agreement, about what the term denotes. In the light of a growing focus on early years provision as preparation for school, TACTYC commissioned a critical review of the underlying perspectives behind the school readiness debate and research evidence that can inform it (Bingham and Whitebread 2012). This book draws on that report and acts as a guide to how research evidence can be translated in day-to-day practice to provide the holistic and balanced approach needed for young children during these crucial years. Considerable portions of the research evidence discussed in

Chapters 2 and 3 are taken directly from the report; where it has been necessary to summarise findings for the sake of accessibility, reference is made to the particular section of Bingham and Whitebread (2012).

Structure of the book

Readiness is not a new concept. During my own teacher training in the early 1970s there was a strong focus on pre-reading and pre-writing activities, influenced by the *Plowden Report* (CACE 1967), to support 'reading readiness'. Lady Plowden, however, also emphasised that a school is 'a community in which children learn to live first and foremost as children and not as future adults' (p. 187). The focus on childhoods to be valued in the present rather than viewed as preparation for future employment meant readiness for school was seen in terms of developmental readiness, recognising that children's physical, social and emotional development must be sufficiently mature to cope with the challenges of school and institutionalised learning. Over the past four decades there has been a shift in understanding as readiness has changed from a primarily maturational definition to a more socially constructed concept (UNICEF 2012). Discussion is now frequently framed in terms of 'readiness to learn' or 'readiness for school', terms that rest on the assumption of formalised academic content. Associated with this are instrumental models of teaching as transmission and learning as reproduction of knowledge. These carry the suggestion that children are passive recipients of information who only learn what they are taught. Increasing demands for children's higher performance creates pressure to prepare young children for later school achievement, leading to tensions between play-based pedagogies and an emphasis on cognitive skills, particularly in literacy and numeracy. School readiness now signifies contradictory messages and the phrase reflects variance in definition and conceptual understanding between policy-makers, educators, academics and educational advisory groups in England. The net effect of the 'potential uses and misuses of the term' (Dockett and Perry 2002) is leading to escalating tension as we talk at cross-purposes.

Between the ages of three and five years, young children develop the social skills and language that underpin all future learning. Progress at school builds on earlier learning in a cumulative manner – for example, learning to read requires a working vocabulary that each child has been developing since birth. Later mathematical ability builds on young children's experiences with shape, size and number gained in handling concrete objects. Without proper understanding of the foundations of children's learning there is a very real danger that this process may be misinterpreted as a need for formal instruction and early introduction to abstract, disembedded knowledge. These issues are explored in Chapter 2 focusing on young children's phenomenal learning abilities as they develop processes of reasoning from their first weeks of life. Establishment of executive functions, such as working memory, inner thought and motivation – crucial to successful learning – are considered. In Chapter 3 attention turns to how young children's drive to learn can be supported, including examination of appropriate pedagogical approaches for teaching and learning in early years classrooms.

Pressure in England for the earliest possible start to formal schooling goes against the grain of international evidence and practice and is educationally counter-productive (Alexander 2010). This situation is unlikely to change in the near future, so thought must be given to how schools can best provide for the social and educational needs of young children regardless of age or level of development. A deficit view of readiness that focuses on what children should 'know' and be able to do at the start of school runs the risk of neglecting children's latent potential. This is particularly likely to occur with children from minority backgrounds or low-income families where attention directed to what they are perceived to lack can result in individual capabilities being neglected or overlooked. Chapter 4 examines the diversity of children in Britain today to look at the implications of background, culture and socio-economic circumstances in light of intervention policies designed to deliver young children to school in a state of readiness. The importance of the home as children's first and foremost learning environment and parents' involvement in their children's learning is discussed.

Chapter 5 picks up on some of the issues already raised in respect of starting school to consider young children's experiences of transition. Although the Reception class is officially part of the Early Years Foundation Stage and subject to the EYFS curriculum, downward pressure exerted by the National Curriculum increasingly leads to pedagogical approaches unsuited to the early age that children begin school. Conflict between active learning approaches and formal academic content is discussed in relation to both Reception and Year 1 classes.

Finally, Chapter 6 draws all these elements together to examine how we might build on strengths in the UK system from a research-informed position. Challenges and concerns are summarised and a range of points to consider are raised in relation to the direction of future policy and practices. Current emphasis within policy (and too frequently in practice also) is on ensuring that young children are ready for school. An opposing perspective suggests it might be more appropriate to ask if schools are ready for four-year-olds (Rogers and Rose 2007). This chapter diverges from both positions in proposing a dynamic systems model as a more contextually relevant way to consider school readiness. Reconceptualising readiness from an ecological perspective acknowledges children's own agency and is sensitive to their environments, culture and communities. The model put forward here is offered as a more helpful alternative to entrenched positions of 'ready children' versus 'ready schools'.

A child only begins school once in a lifetime and it is an event surrounded by mixed feelings – excitement, nervous anticipation and a little apprehension perhaps. From the parents' perspective there is likely to be a sense of pride tinged with sadness that their small child is joining the outside world as an independent individual. If things do not go well, there will never be a second chance to get it right and the impact of those first experiences reverberates for many years. On the other hand, a well-planned transition that meets children's needs, builds on previous experiences and gives them opportunities to develop a positive self-concept as autonomous and capable learners will set the foundations for lifelong learning. For the Reception teacher, it is an immense privilege to work with these very young children as they set out on their school career and teachers are very conscious of the great responsibility this entails. In addition, however, they are likely to be aware of the tensions inherent in their role as they seek to balance the needs of young and vulnerable learners with legislated expectations and requirements. Whilst they will have a good understanding of how young children require active, hands-on learning opportunities and a playful pedagogy within contexts which are personally meaningful to them, teachers are also subject to pressures from above to introduce ever more formal approaches to ensure children achieve set targets. Meanwhile, in preschool settings, nursery classes and kindergartens, early years teachers juggle with similar conflicts as official policy increasingly suggests that children should be made 'ready for school'. Balancing these demands can present a serious challenge for those with young children's welfare and well-being at heart (Andrew 2015). This book explores the many issues involved in the concept of readiness and offers suggestions for a more effective service for children, practitioners and parents.

A few words about terminology

The early years can be a minefield of contradictory or ambiguous language. There is currently a lack of clarity (to say nothing of disparity in status, pay and conditions) between *qualified teachers* and *early years teachers*. The differences are discussed in Chapter 6 but it should be noted that, unless otherwise stipulated, this book uses *teacher* or *early years teacher* to refer to all those who work in a teaching capacity with young children regardless of whether or not they hold Qualified Teacher Status (QTS). *Practitioner* is used as a generic term to cover a wide range of roles across the sector as a whole. It is recognised that all adults are engaged in 'teaching' relationships with young children. It should also be noted that teaching covers a wide range of pedagogical interactions and so should not be taken to imply direct instruction.

Mention of *preschool* should also be explained. Whilst I am aware that some people dislike the term and consider it a disparaging value judgement, it is used here for the sake of convenience. Under-fives attend a confusing variety of early years provision including kindergartens, nursery schools, nursery classes, private nurseries and childminder settings. *Preschool* is intended as an umbrella term to signify any early education experiences outside the home, prior to statutory schooling. The suffix *pre* carries no suggestion of preparation for something else – as the book makes abundantly clear!

References

Alexander, R. (2010) *Children, their World, their Education: Final report and recommendation of the Cambridge Primary Review*, London: Routledge.

Andrew, Y. (2015) What we feel and what we do: emotional capital in early childhood work, *Early Years*, Vol 35 (4): 351–365.

Bingham, S. and Whitebread, D. (2012) *School Readiness: A critical review of perspectives and evidence*. Report prepared for TACTYC available at www.tactyc.org/projects/. Accessed June 25, 2016.

Central Advisory Council for Education (CACE) (1967) *Children and their primary schools* (The Plowden Report), London: HMSO.

Dockett, S. and Perry, B. (2002) Who's ready for what? Young children starting school, *Contemporary Issues in Early Childhood*, Vol 3 (1): 67–89.

Rogers, S. and Rose, J. (2007) Ready for Reception? The advantages and disadvantages of single-point entry to school, *Early Years*, Vol 27 (1): 47–63.

UNICEF (2012) *School Readiness: A conceptual framework*, New York: United Nations Children's Fund.

1

POLICY AND DISCOURSES

Introduction

A large body of research exists, from the UK and elsewhere, to support practitioners and policy-makers in ensuring provision for our youngest children is appropriate and effective. This evidence demonstrates that the 'earlier is better' approach advocated in many official policy documents is misguided, not only because it does not lead to improved outcomes in the long term but also because it is likely to have harmful short-term and long-term consequences (Bingham and Whitebread 2012: section 2.4).

This chapter traces recent policy direction to examine the growing notion of school readiness, the assumptions that underlie such language and the implications raised for all involved in the education and care of young children. It will examine the ambiguity of readiness as a construct to evaluate how the term is used in an attempt to illuminate what it means for children to be ready for school. Finally consideration is given to compulsory school starting age in the UK relative to practice elsewhere to debate whether it is the age that children enter school or the nature of school practices themselves that should be re-evaluated.

It is worth noting that, whilst the focus of this book is on policy and practice in the United Kingdom, this does not necessarily imply a unified approach across the four nations of the UK. England, Scotland, Wales and Northern Ireland all differ to some extent in their approach to early years education and over the first decades of the twenty-first century developed increasingly varied policies (McDowall Clark 2016). Many of the issues raised apply equally across the UK; however, differences are made explicit where they are noteworthy, as indeed are comparisons with other countries from whom, despite considerable variation in school starting ages, there is much to learn.

Recent policy direction and the notion of school readiness

The evidence base supporting the crucial importance of children's early years has fed into recent reviews informing government policy (Field 2010; Marmot 2010; Allen 2011; Tickell 2011). From these it might be surmised that official policy directives emerge directly from research evidence. Such a conclusion is not strictly inaccurate, but the assumption that policy-making is a logical and reasoned process of evaluating evidence and formulating policy as a result would be mistaken. In reality the development of policy is a far more complex phenomenon and economic factors, political interests and ideology all affect what evidence is taken up, how information is interpreted and the action decided as a result (Ball 2006).

The beginning of the twenty-first century saw unprecedented investment in early years provision as part of the Labour government's drive to tackle poverty and reduce social inequality. During this period, amongst other initiatives, *The Children Act* (DfES 2004), incorporating the *Every Child Matters* agenda, emphasised the importance of an integrated approach to services for young children and their families with a subsequent need for multiprofessional, interagency working; the Early Years Foundation Stage (EYFS) was introduced as a discrete phase from birth to five years of age (DfES 2007); and workforce development was highlighted as a crucial element of quality provision. In 2006, the Childcare Act formalised the drive towards professionalisation by establishing graduate Early Years Professional Status (EYPS) and introduced a duty for Local Authorities to close the attainment gap between the least and most disadvantaged children by increasing access to integrated provision. This legislation explicitly encouraged increasing marketisation as a means of extending provision although this has since been challenged as a means of providing sustainable childcare in disadvantaged areas (Lloyd 2012). Additionally, the presence of a large for-profit sector in preschool provision makes it particularly difficult to upgrade the workforce in terms of qualifications and pay levels (Bennett 2012).

Following a general election with no clear majority, a Conservative and Liberal Democrat Coalition (2010–2015) held office until a Conservative government came to power in 2015. Over this period the strong focus on early years education established by the Labour administration was maintained with increasing market economy emphasis. Policy shifted from an aspiration for universal services towards targeted provision, stressing the need for children from deprived backgrounds to be 'made ready' for school, a strongly interventionist strategy advocated by the *Allen Review* (Allen 2011). Within the first few weeks in office the Children's Minister announced a review of the EYFS stating the need 'to shift the focus to getting children ready for education' (Teather 2010), an orientation reinforced the following year in the policy document *Supporting Families in the Foundation Years* (DfE 2011). This set out the Coalition government's response to the *Field Report* on poverty and life chances (2010), the *Allen Review* regarding early intervention (2011) and the *Tickell Review* of the EYFS (2011). Proposals included slimming down the EYFS; introducing a developmental review at age two; plans to extend the 15 hours funded childcare entitlement to the most deprived two-year-olds; bringing EYPs

under the remit of the Teaching Agency and commissioning a review of the qualifications framework. Few recommendations from this review (Nutbrown 2012)
have been accepted outright and the government response – *More Great Childcare:
Raising Quality and Giving Parents More Choice* (DfE 2013) – proved controversial
with a strong challenge to proposed changes in ratios. Replacement of EYPS with
Early Years Teacher Status failed to address very different status and working conditions in comparison to Qualified Teacher Status (QTS).

Some of the actions undertaken by the Coalition, such as reviewing the EYFS
after its first few years of operation and developing provision for two-year-olds,
were measures already proposed by the previous Labour government; it can be
assumed however that the form they took under the new administration had
a different slant in response to the incoming government's priorities. Over this
period the terms 'school readiness' and 'readiness for school' began to be heard
with increasing frequency and with greater emphasis on academic learning. As the
Coalition government had been Conservative-dominated, there was considerable
continuity in policy direction after the Conservatives came to power with a slim
majority in 2015. This suggests that the current drive towards early intervention
within a targeted services ideology is likely to continue for the foreseeable future.

Investment in children

The policy initiatives outlined above have been in response to national and
international concerns and are inevitably driven by economic interests rather than
educational or developmental ones. Investment in Early Childhood Education and
Care (ECEC) is increasingly recognised as generating a high rate of return by laying
the foundations for better student performance, less poverty, more equitable outcomes and greater labour market success (OECD 2006). This is particularly the case
for disadvantaged children and it is argued that access to affordable childcare enables
mothers to return to work thereby helping families out of poverty whilst simultaneously increasing tax income and cutting expenditure on welfare. In recent years
globalisation has also had an impact as ECEC has become regarded as an investment strategy to support international competition. Again returns on investment are
highest in the early years so that the Economist Intelligence Unit (2012) suggests, as
economies increasingly compete on the quality of their human capital, policy-makers
'need to invest in all their people as early in life as possible' (p. 31). Whereas increased
availability of childcare is sufficient to promote parents' (and especially mothers')
involvement in the labour market, high quality settings with an educational focus
are necessary to develop human capital, so the overall policy trajectory has been to
focus on both quantity and quality of ECEC provision. Whether ECEC is envisaged
as a present or future benefit, however, a human capital perspective positions young
children as objects of national investment. A corollary of this is that early years provision, and indeed education in general, rather than focusing on children's present
development and learning, is primarily viewed as a means to cultivate economically productive citizens. This has subsequent effects on curriculum and assessment as

outcomes such as numeracy and literacy skills, perceived as fundamentally important for employment, are unduly emphasised (Sims and Waniganayake 2015).

Recent English policy documents and reports echo these discourses in making explicit an official perspective of early years education as a national investment that can pay dividends for society as a whole, for instance:

> [T]his government is determined to ensure that the system delivers high quality at good value for children, parents and the tax-payer.
>
> (Elizabeth Truss, Foreword to More Great Childcare, DfE 2013)

> More great childcare is vital to ensuring we can compete in the global race, by helping parents back to work and readying children for school and, eventually employment.
>
> (DfE 2013: 6)

> Through Early Intervention the next and succeeding generations could be prepared and made ready for school, for work, for parenthood and for life itself.
>
> (Allen 2011: 6)

Such a focus on future employability leads to a specific view of ECEC. This is evident in the EYFS, the stated purpose of which is to 'promote teaching and learning to ensure children's "school readiness" and give children the broad range of knowledge and skills that provide the right foundation for good future progress through school and life' (DfE 2014: 5). Faulkner and Coates (2013) suggest that the overriding aim of the revised EYFS is to prepare children for school and they raise additional concerns that extending education to two-year-olds is likely to lead to further 'schoolification' of childhood. Indeed whilst various and contradictory uses of the term 'school readiness' are increasingly cited by politicians, policy-makers and advisers to government, the scope of the government's policies is affecting younger and younger children. The *Allen Review* (2011) on early intervention, for instance, suggests that 'all children should have regular assessment of their development from birth to age five … so that they can be put on the path to "school readiness"' (p. 56).

Emphasis on preparation for school is not just a concern in the UK but has become increasingly widespread (Kaga et al. 2010). As governments around the world look to early childhood services to prepare children for formal education there is greater focus on assessment and academic learning goals that threatens to devalue important, holistic educational experiences for young children (Ang 2014). Whilst the phrase 'school readiness' or 'readiness for school' is used with a variety of connotations in policy documents and reports, in parallel it is used to different ends by academics and educational advisory groups. The arguments surfacing about whether, how and why a child should be 'made ready' are symptomatic of the far deeper tension growing within the early years education sector and a deep conceptual divide.

What is readiness? Definitions and contradictions

The readiness debate has been aggravated by conflation of two distinct concepts: *readiness to learn* and *readiness for school*. Learning is innate and all children, at all ages, are ready to learn, so the significant question is not *whether* a child is ready to learn, but rather *what* a child is ready to learn. Child developmentalists use the notion of readiness in relation to developmental levels; these indicate the point at which an individual has theoretical capacity to learn a skill or develop an area of understanding, based on the average age that ability occurs. In this sense readiness relates to domains of physical development, intellectual ability, social and emotional maturity and health, but rates of development are affected by many factors leading to considerable variation. *Readiness for school* is a more finite construct (Kagan 2007) suggesting a fixed standard of physical, intellectual and social development that enables children to learn in a structured learning environment. It implies that young children should meet the requirements of school and be able to assimilate the curriculum so the term typically embraces specific cognitive and linguistic skills.

Readiness for school used to be considered a straightforward matter involving basic independence skills, such as being able to go to the toilet and dress oneself unaided, alongside a level of social and emotional maturity evident in playing alongside other children or sharing an adult's attention. Such criteria are now viewed as a 'minimum requirement' (Wilsher 2014) and since the Education Reform Act introduced the *National Curriculum for England and Wales* in 1988, expectations of young children have escalated. Over this time a growing tension has arisen between policy-makers, practitioners and academics about the nature of school readiness with considerable disagreement about what the term signifies and how it should be interpreted.

Although the National Curriculum only applies to children of compulsory school age, comprehensive restructuring of the educational system has inevitably had an effect upon programmes for younger children, resulting in what Blenkin and Kelly termed 'the death of infancy'.

> For the effect of the National Curriculum on infant education has been …
> to destroy the concept of infancy, to remove it from the vocabulary and the
> discourse of the educational debate, and thus to eliminate any notion that
> the educational requirements of children 5–7 are in any fundamental sense
> different from those of 16 year olds. (Blenkin and Kelly 1994: 3)

As National Curriculum assessments impacted on schools, 'infants' became 'Key Stage 1 pupils' and the pressures of accountability increased demands placed on them to provide evidence that investment in early years education pays dividends in terms of improved outcomes. This growing focus on curricular accountability within primary schools has altered notions of what school readiness is, thereby affecting provision for under-fives (Pianta et al. 2007). Although the importance of rounded development is clearly identified as a key aspect of school readiness within documents such as the *Allen Review*, the *EYFS* and *More Great Childcare*, the term is too often associated with formal, academic knowledge and this interpretation endangers provision of appropriate learning experiences and opportunities for young children. Rogers and Rose (2007) argue that though the concept of school readiness may seem to imply a developmental rationale, potential flaws of misjudgement by those making the evaluation have rendered it controversial, an argument supported by recent research indicating that parents, teachers and childcare professionals interpret the term in a way that is in stark contrast to that used by policy-makers and regulators (PACEY 2013).

UNICEF (2012) suggest that the simplicity of the term 'school readiness' belies the complexity of the concept and no doubt this is behind the wide-ranging uses of the term within official discourse. The term is often used to apply to skills considered necessary in order to benefit from schooling, but may also refer to a bank of knowledge deemed valuable for young children to acquire and the prescription of how and when they should be expected to demonstrate this. In this way, economic and social reasons serve as a basis for interpreting the concept as readiness for lifelong learning but at the same time it is used to determine and direct goals for the early years curriculum and teaching methods. As a result, school readiness is variously promoted as a benefit to children themselves, to schools and to national interests although clearly each beneficiary's gain is dependent on the meaning attributed to the term. For instance the *Field Report* suggests that:

> Greater equality of school readiness would make teaching, particularly in the first few years of primary school, easier and more productive. Overall, this means that it is highly productive to invest in disadvantaged young children. (2010: 40)

Tickell (2011: 19) attempted to avoid 'the more ambiguous and emotive connotations' by raising the notion of *unreadiness* although, by drawing on evidence that children behind in their development at age five are likely to still be behind their peers at age seven, familiar concerns are reinforced about risks for children who are not ready. The readiness debate is often accompanied by warnings that imply if a child is perceived by their primary school teacher as behind, then they will experience problems fitting in to school. Use of the phrase 'behind in their development' could be argued to present an over-simplified view that fails to recognise that development is uneven and multi-dimensional. A young child's level of development varies across different domains so children are not likely to achieve levels considered important for school success in all domains at the same time.

Government expectations that children should be *made ready* for the established primary school system and Year 1 curriculum are evident in the clear association between the EYFS and school readiness. The Statutory Framework starts out by defining 'what providers must do … to promote the learning and development of all children in their care, and to ensure they are ready for school'

(DfE 2014: paragraph 1.1). There is significant potential for confusion here because a combination of policy changes over recent years, such as single point entry into Reception class in the September following a child's fourth birthday, and use of the phrase 'ready for school', has led to multiple interpretations of when a child actually starts school. Ofsted (2014) found ambiguity about whether children start their school career at the beginning of Reception class or not until Year 1. Misunderstandings arise because, although statutory school starting age is five years (or the term following their fifth birthday), in practice most children enter Reception up to a year before statutory school age, exceptionally young in comparison to their counterparts in most other countries. As Tickell (2011) acknowledged, the start of Reception at age four is what most parents and carers recognise as the beginning of school life although this actually still lies within the Early Years Foundation Stage curriculum with its emphasis on developmentally-appropriate methods of teaching and learning through play. The EYFS (DfE 2014: paragraph 1.8) implies this is a transition year when children are prepared for entry into Year 1 – but if Reception is also understood as the start of school it leaves opens the possibility that children should be prepared for this change at the age of four.

Alternative models of school readiness

The concept of school readiness is complex, embracing many components, and as the idea gains currency globally, an increasing number of definitions have emerged (UNICEF 2012). School readiness, as understood by teachers, early years practitioners and academics in the field, is a concept that lays less emphasis on what children know but focuses instead on independence and self-reliance. Few teachers rate reading, writing and arithmetic skills as important factors in being ready for school and the majority of professionals define school readiness as having strong social skills; being able to cope emotionally with being separated from parents and carers; achieving relative independence in personal care and having a curiosity about the world and disposition to learn (PACEY 2013).

The majority of definitions of school readiness place the onus for school readiness on children, focusing on skills and competencies observable within the child. This is true of both maturational models (i.e. those that focus on achieving a certain level of cognitive, socio-emotional and psychomotor development) and environmental views equating readiness for school with identifiable learning, such as knowledge of colours and being able to count. Whilst maturationist perspectives are biological and rest on the notion of natural processes that cannot be hastened, environmental definitions assume universal, measurable criteria. This latter model would enable skills and knowledge that children lack to be identified and taught to produce school readiness (Dockett and Perry 2002).

Other definitions take a broader perspective such as constructivist models that recognise schools as artificial environments where children are instructed in specific skill sets for future life (Snow 2006). From this perspective, efforts to prepare children for school must take account of expectations from the community, including parents, professional educators and policy-makers, providing the sort of environments that foster relevant abilities. A more multi-directional, ecological model recognises that school readiness is the product of interaction between individuals, families and systems thus highlighting the relationship between children and their environments. This shifts the focus of readiness onto schools, emphasising the need for schools to adapt to children's developmental needs, taking account of aspects of the environment that can encourage or hinder learning (Kaga 2008). 'Readiness' here is understood as the match, or fit, between children's individual readiness and the readiness of the environments in which they are expected to learn and develop. This broader conceptualisation, regarding readiness as a condition of institutions as well as individuals, is increasingly being adopted by advisory groups and early years experts (Graue 2006) and is the basis for the model of school readiness set out in Chapter 6.

Assessing school readiness: Intervention and purpose

As early years provision is more and more framed in terms of preparation for formal schooling, anxiety about children's school readiness grows in magnitude. Ofsted (2014) laments the fact no agreed definition of school readiness exists, but, given the range of perspectives across different interest groups, attempting to reach such agreement would be extremely difficult. For governments of all persuasions however, efforts to achieve short-term political goals are based on an assumption that effective education can be measured and that legislating for changes in a pre-school curriculum will lead to higher quality teaching and learning, resulting in higher outcomes for children. This brings the notion of school readiness into sharp focus and raises questions of how it might be monitored. Narrow pre-primary approaches, such as those adopted in England (OECD 2006), prioritise literacy and numeracy skills in order to smoothly align to primary school curricular goals. This encourages a model of readiness focused on what children know rather than their individual development, contrasting starkly with perspectives that focus on contexts and environments to support development.

The *Field Report* (2010) recommends monitoring school readiness through specific tests, an approach endorsed by the report into early intervention (Allen 2011). The measure identified (the *Bracken School Readiness Assessment Tests*) covers six basic skills of colour recognition; letter identification (lower and upper case); numbers and counting; vocabulary related to size; shape identification and ability to make comparisons by matching or differentiating between objects. Many other similar developmental checklists are available but there is danger in assuming that testing skills in isolation can give a clear picture of children's ability (Snow 2006). In addition, all such tests are essentially normative as they are created to enable comparison between 'typical' five-year-olds.

Emphasis on reaching targets requires assessment and Pascal and Bertram (2000) remind us that we live in an audited society where what is measurable is seen as significant. They warn of the importance of ensuring what is measured has real significance rather than simply focussing on things that are easily measured.

Assessing school readiness through measures such as the Bracken test derives from an environmental perspective that looks to screen children's knowledge and ability, putting programmes in place to directly teach what they are perceived to lack. This deficit model is behind targeted interventions that assume the home environment fails in providing sufficient stimulation to develop school readiness. It focuses on those aspects of readiness that can be taught, an approach that raises concerns about 'schoolification' (OECD 2006; Alexander 2010). In contrast, a maturational model, constructing readiness as a way of being that cannot be taught, rests on very different assumptions and is a perspective more typically applied to white, middle-class children (Graue 2006).

Assessments of school readiness are prone to emphasise outcomes rather than learning processes. As a result, interventions that focus on enabling children to achieve certain outcomes, rather than fostering effective learning, are liable to simply encourage them to produce the expected answers. Bennett (2005) warns against too great an emphasis on academic goals but also cautions against excessive suspicion of schoolification and reluctance to orient children towards learning goals valued by parents, schools and society. Orienting children towards learning goals does not mean they should be subjected to over-formalised academic programmes but necessitates opportunities to master the skills of learning in its wider sense. This implies a very different understanding about the purpose of schools and what primary education is for.

The Cambridge Primary Review (Alexander 2010) argues that the aims of primary education have long been confused or tokenistic with curriculum following a much narrower path than its proclaimed aims. The review calls for a coherent set of aims to drive curriculum, pedagogy and school life and proposes an evidence-grounded framework responsive to the imperatives of childhood, society and the wider world. The confused aims and different understandings of the purpose of early education identified by the Cambridge Primary Review Trust lie behind the miscellaneous interpretations of school readiness. There is no agreement on a definition of the term 'school readiness' or 'readiness for school' and its use because there is no agreement on what young children should be prepared for (if, indeed they should be prepared for anything). In essence, disagreement about terminology and definition encapsulates a fundamental difference in conception of the purpose of early years education.

The question of school starting age

Recently the issue of school readiness has received particular attention within the UK due to the exceptionally early age when British children enter statutory schooling. In most other countries children begin school at six, or even seven years of age: the statutory school starting age in Britain is five. Moreover, since the 1990s the practice of entering children into the Reception class from age four has become increasingly prevalent. Such an early start to school has always been surrounded by controversy (Cleave and Brown 1991) but in recent years, where a focus on getting children ready for school at an earlier and earlier age has combined with the political drive for more formal approaches, it has become an issue of serious concern to many people.

It might be expected that decisions about beginning school would be based on what is most beneficial for children. Rogers and Rose (2007) point out however that this has not necessarily been the guiding force behind policy-making in the UK. The school age was set at five in the 1870 Foster Education Act; at the time the decision had no educational rationale but was a compromise between different interest groups. Age five was agreed partly in response to concerns about children's welfare, but also to appease powerful economic lobbies who believed that the sooner children began education the sooner it might be over so they could enter the labour market. Thus the notion of young children as a national investment has been central to policy-making from the beginning of state-funded education (McDowall Clark 2016). Whilst Sharp (2002) affirms that there are no convincing grounds for a school starting age of five, nor the practice of admitting four-year-olds into Reception classes, school entry remains early, possibly because of (mis)perceived ideas of the educational benefits but also due to lack of affordable childcare. This is the reason an early start to school is preferred by many parents (Blake and Finch 2000).

Comparison with other countries highlights the extent to which Britain is out of step with the rest of the world. UNESCO statistics indicate that globally approximately 10 per cent of countries have a starting age of five years (World Bank 2014). Amongst these are Australia, New Zealand, Pakistan and several island groups mainly in the Caribbean. The most common age to begin primary school is six years as seen across Western Europe, the USA and most of South America, Africa, the Arab States and East Asia. Within Eastern Europe and Central Asia, as well as in Russia, China and Brazil, seven is generally the starting age. Although there is variation across the UK, the age of starting school is younger than these international norms in each of the UK nations. It is particularly early for children in Northern Ireland who, at four years old, have a younger start than any other country. Whilst the majority of children in England and Wales begin school considerably earlier than necessary, the compulsory starting age is not until the term following a child's fifth birthday. The most flexible school entry system in the UK is Scotland where possibility of deferral makes it unusual for children to begin school before the age of four years, six months. Table 1.1 illustrates the comparison between the UK and other countries of the European Union. From this table it can be seen that whilst the British starting age of five is already unusual, the fact that most children are accepted into school from the age of four makes the discrepancy more extreme.

Comparisons are fraught with difficulties because so many contextual factors impinge on children's experiences and educational outcomes. The situation is muddled by accepted practice in some countries, such as Britain, for parents to choose to send children to school before statutory starting age. In addition, as Moss (2013) points out, the fact that some countries such as Poland and Hungary have made the later stage of early years education compulsory is blurring the distinction between

TABLE 1.1 School starting ages in Europe (European Commission/Eurydice 2015;World Bank 2014)

N. Ireland	Age 4
Cyprus, England, Malta, Netherlands Scotland, Wales	Age 5
Austria, Belgium, Croatia, Czech Republic, Denmark, France, Germany, Greece, Hungary, Iceland, Republic of Ireland, Italy, Liechtenstein, Luxembourg, Norway, Poland, Portugal, Romania, Slovakia, Slovenia, Spain, Switzerland, Turkey	Age 6
Bulgaria, Estonia, Finland, Latvia, Lithuania, Serbia, Sweden	Age 7

early childhood and compulsory education. Nevertheless, it is instructive to consider alternative approaches so as to gain a wider perspective on the effects of different practices. Though few countries begin at such an early age as the UK, there is ample evidence to attest to their better long-term results by age 11 (OECD 2006; Rogers and Rose 2007). The reason for this is most likely that children in the UK frequently begin formal schooling before they are developmentally ready to cope with academic content. The rationale for early entry to school is intended to benefit children at risk of school failure and is a major part of policy initiatives to 'narrow the gap' (Field 2010; Allen 2011). Whilst formal instruction at an early age can show some initial gains, in the long term these do not last (Sharp 2002) because children are not sufficiently developmentally mature to benefit from direct teaching of literacy or numeracy skills. Kavkler et al. (2000) suggest that, rather than providing a strong start by beginning formal scholastic skills early, 'the English educational system appears simply to confirm, if not confer, failure for low achievers thereby *increasing* variation between children' (p. 83, emphasis in original). Studies of English children's achievements in both literacy and numeracy show no long-term gains when compared to their counterparts in other parts of the world such as Slovenia (Kavkler et al. 2000), Japan (Whitburn 2000) and New Zealand (Suggate 2007). It is evident that children who begin formal education at a later stage invariably catch up and acquire skills rapidly.

Comparatively short-lived gains are also counterbalanced by negative consequences for young children's emotional and educational well-being. This is particularly marked for children from minority and/or low-income backgrounds many of whom would benefit from more personalised attention and support for learning in smaller groups (Bennett 2013). Young children who begin formal schooling before they are developmentally mature are more at risk of mental health problems (Browning and Heinesen 2007) and the younger children start school, the more likely they are to be diagnosed with Attention Deficit Hyperactive Disorder (ADHD) (Elder 2010). This is because starting school later provides greater opportunities for the sort of playful learning that supports young children's communication skills, disposition towards learning and ability to regulate their own behaviour, whereas anxiety, lack of self-esteem and poor motivation are all associated with formal demands at too young an age. Dee and Sievertsen (2015) suggest that a one-year increase in school starting age benefits young children by allowing greater exposure to early childhood environments and leads to significantly improved mental health.

Concerns about young children's immaturity and the difficulties they may consequently encounter can sometimes lead to deferral or a delay in entry to education for specific individuals. This practice of keeping the youngest children out of kindergarten for a year to enable them to catch up in their development (referred to as 'redshirting' in America) is prevalent in the USA and Chile but unusual in Britain where parents have to make a special request with no guarantee of it being agreed. Where this practice does occur it is mostly boys who are kept back, showing the prevalence of maturational concepts as no evidence suggests any gender differentiation in readiness for school (Snow 2006). Benefits of deferral are mixed however (Sharp et al. 2009). Marking out some children as immature may inadvertently prevent certain developmental delays or disabilities from being recognised and receiving appropriate support. Nor is it a satisfactory answer in the long term as difficulties may arise later when children reach an age where they can leave statutory education. A more appropriate response would be to focus on the character of early years provision rather than school starting age and reconsider the provision available when children enter the school system.

The nature of early education

Although children in most other countries start formal schooling between one and three years later than in the UK, those children nonetheless benefit from various forms of early education, the majority attending preschools and kindergartens. It is the sort of educational experiences they encounter that makes a crucial difference and impacts on later educational success. Certainly young children are not 'ready' to sit at desks doing paper-and-pencil activities for long periods of time at four, five or perhaps even six years of age, but they *can* benefit from all kinds of appropriately implemented education. The question to be asked, therefore, is not what age children should begin school, nor what they should know and be able to do when they get there. Instead we should be asking what schools need to do to meet the needs of the children who walk through their doors and what sort of educational experiences should be offered. It is not uncommon for example, for young children in Wales to begin school from the age of three, but the Foundation Phase curriculum covering educational provision for three- to seven-year-olds is play-based in line with children's natural learning strategies. In England the increasing development of targeted intervention means that many children will begin to attend provision in a school building from age two, so a clear, conceptual difference must be made between 'starting to go to school' and 'starting to be formally schooled'. Notions of school readiness, therefore, need to take account of the pedagogical transition from a child-led, play-based curriculum to a more teacher-led, instructional approach.

This transition from one form of learning to another has become an issue of contention as many involved with early years education become increasingly concerned about schoolification of preschool provision through employment of primary school methods and content (OECD 2006). Learning for young children needs to be active and experiential to support curiosity, enabling the development of confidence in their own learning rather than, as school readiness might imply, achieving predetermined levels of knowledge. Unfortunately, too often the idea of school carries with it expectations of didactic instruction and academic content so that the idea of children learning through play is viewed with suspicion or as a frivolous indulgence. Katz (2010) suggests that the apparent dichotomy between formal academic learning and spontaneous play activities is misleading and makes a distinction instead between *academic* and *intellectual* educational goals. Katz argues that children's readiness for school has too often been seen in terms of academic goals, leading to instruction in literacy and numeracy skills. This simply encourages children to acquire discrete bits of disembedded information instead of learning that evolves from their previous knowledge and skills. Academic goals prize the ability to give correct answers above understanding, requiring young children to memorise facts divorced from any meaningful context. Intellectual goals on the other hand, involve reasoning and children making their own hypotheses and predictions in their search for understanding. Intellectual goals motivate young children to master academic skills such as reading, writing, measuring and counting as they follow their interests because they see the purpose and value of these skills. Katz (2010) suggests that we tend to overestimate children academically and underestimate them intellectually. This claim seems borne out by the current situation in England where increasing emphasis is given to formal activities and direct instruction at the expense of opportunities for children to develop their own ideas and make sense of their environments through activities that engage and absorb them.

High quality early education that enables children to explore and investigate focuses on *how* children learn rather than *what* they learn (Stewart 2011). Children's approach to learning can be observed through the characteristics of effective learning set out in the EYFS framework. Characteristics of effective learning – playing and exploring, active learning and creating and thinking critically – involve such traits as demonstrating curiosity and persistence, and the ability to concentrate despite distractions and to solve problems. Reception classrooms that foster these capacities by offering young children meaningful learning contexts where they can make choices, try out different strategies and learn from mistakes enable children to engage in learning at their own pace. This makes the question of precise starting age less critical. Such provision supports positive learning dispositions, motivation and the ability to regulate their own behaviour – all aspects that are fundamental to later school success.

Conclusion

The school readiness debate stretches far beyond those young children on the brink of starting school and the adults who are involved with them – ripples and repercussions of the readiness agenda affect *all* young children as official public perceptions increasingly shift towards viewing them as school pupils in the making. Readiness is now the dominant narrative that shapes relationships across all parts of the education system (Moss 2013). Extensive research over many decades means that we have a thorough understanding of young children's learning processes, the most supportive environments and the pedagogies that foster motivation and intellectual curiosity – surely the fundamental traits to sustain lifelong learning. Yet children continue to be subjected to inappropriate, narrow and counterproductive expectations that contradict the evidence in an attempt to ensure readiness for school. Graue (2006) suggests that if the answer is readiness, we are still searching for the question and describes this as an ethical responsibility. This book attempts to take up that responsibility; its core substance is not a focus on children's preparation for school – nor even schools' readiness for children – but the proposal of a contextually relevant and dynamic system, one that is sensitive to culture, context and diversity. This reflects the UNICEF (2012) framework that identifies three dimensions to take into account, those of ready *children*, ready *schools* and ready *families*. The dynamic model of readiness set out in Chapter 6 observes each of these elements and provides a conceptual tool to inform dialogue and debate. Young children have only one opportunity to begin school; they need and deserve educational experiences that are purposeful and meaningful, taking place within environments that nurture development and opportunity, alongside responsive adults who value children's own interests and support them in their search for understanding.

References

Alexander, R. (2010) *Children, their world, their education: final report and recommendations of the Cambridge Primary Review*, London: Routledge.

Allen, G. (2011) *Early intervention: the next steps*. London: Cabinet Office.

Ang, L. (2014). Preschool or prep school? Rethinking the role of early years education, *Contemporary Issues in Early Childhood*, Vol 15 (2): 185–199.

Ball, S. J. (2006) *Education, policy and social class*, Abingdon: Routledge.

Bennett, J. (2005) Curriculum issues in national policy making, *European Early Childhood Education Research Journal*, Vol 13 (2): 5–23.

Bennett, J. (2012) *Roma early childhood inclusion: the RECI overview report, a joint initiative of the Open Society Foundations, the Roma Education Fund and UNICEF*, Budapest: OSF/REF/ UNICEF.

Bennett, J. (2013) A response from the co-author of 'a strong and equal partnership', in P. Moss (ed), *Early childhood and compulsory education: reconceptualising the relationship*, London: Sage.

Bingham, S. and Whitebread, D. (2012) *School readiness: a critical review of perspectives and evidence*. Report prepared for TACTYC available at www.tactyc.org/projects/. Accessed June 25, 2016.

Blake, M. and Finch, S. (2000) *Survey of the movement of children from playgroups to reception classes*, London: National Centre for Social Research.

Blenkin, G. and Kelly, A.V. (1994) The death of infancy, *Education 3-13*, Vol 22 (3): 3–9.

Browning, M. and Heinesen, E. (2007) Class size, teacher hours and educational attainment, *The Scandinavian Journal of Economics*, Vol 109 (2): 415–438.

Cleave, S. and Brown, S. (1991) *Early to school: four year olds in infant classes*, London: NFER/ Routledge.

Dee, T. and Sievertsen, H. (2015) *The gift of time? School starting age and mental health*, National Bureau of Economic Research Working Paper no. 2160. Cambridge, MA: NBER.

Department for Education (DfE) (2011) *Supporting families in the Foundation years*, London: DfE.

Department for Education (DfE) (2013) *More great childcare – raising quality and giving parents more choice*, available at www.gov.uk/government/publications/more-great-childcare-raising-quality-and-giving-parents-more-choice. Accessed June 25, 2016.

Department for Education (DfE) (2014) *Statutory framework for the Early Years Foundation Stage*, DFE-00337-2014, London: DfE.

Department for Education and Skills (DfES) (2004) *The children act*, London: HMSO.

Department for Education and Skills (DfES) (2007) *Early Years Foundation Stage*, London: DfES.

Dockett, S. and Perry, B. (2002) Who's ready for what? Young children starting school, *Contemporary Issues in Early Childhood*, Vol 3 (1): 67–89.

Economist Intelligence Unit (EIU) (2012) *Starting well: benchmarking early education across the world*, London: Economist Intelligence Unit, available at www.economistinsights.com/leadership-talent-innovation/analysis/starting-well. Accessed June 25, 2016.

Elder, T. E. (2010) The importance of relative standards in ADHD diagnoses: evidence based on exact birth dates, *Journal of Health Economics*, Vol 29 (5): 641–656.

European Commission/Eurydice (2015) *Compulsory education in Europe: Eurydice facts and figures*, Luxembourg: Publications Office of the European Union.

Faulkner, D. and Coates, E. (2013) Early childhood policy and practice in England: twenty years of change, *International Journal of Early Years Education*, Vol 21 (2/3): 244–263.

Field, F. (2010) *The foundation years: preventing poor children becoming poor adults. The report of the independent review on poverty and life chances*, London: Cabinet Office.

Graue, E. (2006) The answer is readiness: now what is the question?, *Early Education and Development*, Vol 17 (1): 43–56.

Kaga, Y. (2008) *What approaches to linking ECCE and Primary Education?* UNESCO Policy Brief on Early Childhood, no 44, available at http://unesdoc.unesco.org/images/0017/001799/179934e.pdf. Accessed June 25, 2016.

Kaga, Y., Bennett, J. and Moss, P. (2010) *Caring and Learning Together. A cross-national study on the integration of early childhood care and education within education*, Paris: UNESCO.

Kagan, S. L. (2007) Readiness – multiple meanings and perspectives, in M. Woodhead and P. Moss (eds), *Early childhood and primary education transitions in the lives of young children*, available at www.bernardvanleer.org/Early_Childhood_and_Primary_Education_Transitions_in_the_Lives_of_Young_Children. Accessed June 25, 2016.

Katz, L. (2010) STEM in the early years, *Early childhood research and practice*, Fall edition, available at http://ecrp.uiuc.edu/beyond/seed/katz.html. Accessed June 25, 2016.

Kavkler, M., Tancig, S., Magajna, L. and Aubrey, C. (2000) Getting it right from the start? The influence of early school entry on later achievements in mathematics, *European Early Childhood Education Research Journal*, Vol 8 (1): 75–93.

Lloyd, E. (2012) The marketisation of early years education and childcare in England, in L. Miller and D. Hevey (eds), *Policy issues in the early years*, London: Sage.

Marmot, M. (2010) *Fair society, healthy lives. Strategic review of health inequalities in England*, available at www.marmotreview.org.uk. Accessed June 25, 2016.

McDowall Clark, R. (2016) *Childhood in society for the early years* (3rd ed), London: Sage.

Moss, P. (ed) (2013) *Early childhood and compulsory education: reconceptualising the relationship*, Abingdon: Routledge.

Nutbrown, C. (2012) Foundations for quality: the independent review of early education and childcare qualifications. Final Report, available at www.gov.uk/government/publications/nutbrown-review-foundations-for-quality. Accessed June 25, 2016.

Ofsted (2014) *Are you ready? Good practice in school readiness*, available at www.ofsted.gov.uk/resources/140074. Accessed June 25, 2016.

Organisation for Economic Co-operation and Development (OECD) (2006) *Starting strong II: early childhood education and care*, Paris: OECD.

Pascal, C. and Bertram, T. (2000) *Further memorandum from The Effective Early Learning Project (EY 82)*, available at www.publications.parliament.uk/pa/cm199900/cmselect/cmeduemp/386/0061407.htm. Accessed June 25, 2016.

Pianta R., Cox, M. and Snow, K. (eds) (2007) *School readiness and the transition to kindergarten in the era of accountability*, Baltimore, MD: Paul. H. Brookes.

Professional Association for Childcare and Early Years (PACEY) (2013) *What does 'school ready' really mean?* Available at www.pacey.org.uk/Pacey/media/Website-files/school ready/School-Ready-Report.pdf. Accessed June 25, 2016.

Rogers, S. and Rose, J. (2007) Ready for Reception? The advantages and disadvantages of single-point entry to school, *Early Years*, Vol 27 (1): 47–63.

Sharp, C. (2002) *School starting age: European policy and recent research*, Paper presented at the Local Government Association Seminar 'When Should Our Children Start School?', LGA Conference Centre, London, November 1st, Slough: NFER.

Sharp, C., George, N., Sargent, C., O'Donnell, S. and Heron, M. (2009) *International thematic probe: the influence of relative age on learner attainment and development*, London: QCA/NFER.

Sims, M. and Waniganayake, M. (2015) The performance of compliance in early childhood: neoliberalism and nice ladies, *Global Studies of Childhood*, Vol 5 (3): 333–345.

Snow, K. (2006) Measuring school readiness: conceptual and practical considerations, *Early Education and Development*, Vol 17: 7–41.

Stewart, N. (2011) *How children learn: the characteristics of effective learning*, London: Early Education.

Suggate, S. (2007) Research into early reading instruction and Luke Effects in the development of reading, *Journal for Waldorf/Steiner Education*, Vol 11 (2): 17–20.

Teather, S. (2010) *Invitation to Clare Tickell to lead a review into the Early Years Foundation Stage*, Government press release, available at www.gov.uk/government/news/review-of-early-years-foundation-stage. Accessed June 25, 2016.

Tickell, C. (2011) *The early years: foundations for life, health and learning*, available at www.educationengland.org.uk/documents/pdfs/2011-tickell-report-eyfs.pdf. Accessed June 25, 2016.

UNICEF (2012) *School readiness: a conceptual framework*, New York: United Nations Children's Fund.

Whitburn, J. (2000) *Strength in numbers: learning maths in Japan and England*, London: NIESR.

Wilsher, M. (2014) *Unsure start*, Ofsted Early Years Annual Report 2012–2013, available at www.nationalarchives.gov.uk/20141124154759. Accessed June 25, 2016.

World Bank (2014) *Official entrance age to primary education*, available at http://data.worldbank.org/indicator/SE.PRM.AGES. Accessed June 25, 2016.

2

TAKING ACCOUNT OF DEVELOPMENT

Introduction

Any consideration of children's readiness for school – or indeed, readiness to learn – must take account of the child's natural innate development. In the past the concept of readiness to learn was underpinned by Piaget's ideas of developmental stages that assumed children were not ready to learn until they reached a certain stage of development. Subsequent research showed that Piaget severely underestimated the abilities of young children and took little account of the important influence of social interactions and language. Contemporary developmental psychology no longer accepts that there are different developmental stages in children's ability so that they cannot learn until cognitively ready; it is now recognised that young children are limited only by their lack of experience and accumulated knowledge and skills.

Previous educational policy directives, such as the Plowden Report (CACE 1967), were influenced by Piagetian ideas and assumed children only became capable of logical thought based on symbolic and abstract reasoning in adolescence. Today it is accepted that all the basic forms of learning and reasoning are available from infancy. New environments may be challenging because lack of experience makes it difficult for young children to understand situations and work out how to act. But when this becomes clear from the context or through guidance of sympathetic and supportive adults, children's potential for learning is phenomenal. It is now acknowledged that young children are much more capable than was previously believed, beginning life as active, motivated learners.

This chapter examines evidence from cognitive neuroscience research considering what is known about how children's minds develop and the processes of reasoning and understanding that underpin learning. Basic executive functions, such as statistical learning, learning by imitation, learning by analogy and causal reasoning are explained and factors that may support or inhibit their growth are discussed in relation to practice. Young children are competent, active learners from birth and this chapter outlines the specific processes that support typical cognitive development. Within the first few years of life children develop their knowledge base, metacognition and self-regulation (becoming aware of and in control of their own thoughts, emotions and behaviour) and all these have a crucial role in successful learning.

Development of processes for learning

> 6-week-old Jake has just woken and lies in his basket looking around him. His eye is caught by one of the basket handles and he reaches an arm randomly in its direction. His eyes shift from the handle to his hand and back again and he adjusts his hand to be slightly nearer the handle. For five minutes he concentrates hard, gradually correcting the position of his hand until he manages to grasp the handle. He lets go, then reaches out again; this time he can make the adjustments more easily and it takes only a couple of minutes to succeed in his objective. Jake continues to practice, each time fine-tuning his movement till he can reach for the handle directly without hesitation. Losing interest in the activity he calls out for attention.

Over the last 30 years or so, cognitive psychologists have used newly emerging technologies, such as habituation, eye-tracking and computer modelling to reveal an impressive range of processes by which the human brain learns. At the same time, increasingly sophisticated technologies for observation have been developed enabling systematic gathering of data relating to young children's behaviours and actions, and complex analysis of resultant patterns and tendencies. Until recently, these two areas of developmental psychology and neurobiology were studied separately; whereas one is concerned with observation and measurement of behaviour, cognition and emotion, the other concentrates on study of cellular, neurophysiological and biochemical processes in the brain and autonomic nervous system. It is now possible to simultaneously study neurobiological processes accompanying observed behaviour through neurophysiological measures and brain-imaging techniques challenging traditional notions of the relationship between mind and brain. Whilst this brings useful insights into young children's learning, Wastell and White (2012) warn of the potential for neuroscience to medicalise policy discourse, silencing vital moral debate.

Developmental cognitive neuroscience has established that many fundamental processes that underpin thinking, reasoning and learning are already present and fully functioning at birth whilst others become available within the first four to five years of life. During this period, the brain increases in size fourfold, largely as a result of rapid increase in the number of synaptic connections between neurons in the cerebral cortex. Many experiments have shown very early emergence of a range of basic learning processes. Simple forms of the building mechanisms of cognition are present in children soon after birth and processes of statistical learning, learning by imitation, learning by analogy and causal learning emerge within extremely short timespans (Goswami 2015). These support cognitive development and promote rapid learning about social stimuli like faces, physical events (such as Jake's reaching action above) and language. In effect, this research enables redefinition of what is understood by 'early learning'. It is evident that human infants emerge into the world equipped with the systems for active and independent learning from the start.

This learning is innate and automatic; the mechanisms that support brain development are intuitive and may bypass adult caregivers unless particular attention is paid. For instance, in the example above, Jake's systematic learning of how to reach out to an object could easily be unobserved; an adult responding when he called would assume he had just woken and be unaware of the learning accomplished through his methodical activity. Although a wide range of developmental milestones, such as smiling in response to a familiar carer or grasping an object are noted as evidence of appropriate progress, the sophistication of the learning they depend on is not always apparent. Jake had to assess both distance and direction to be able to successfully reach the handle, no easy task with still limited experience of his environment. In addition he needed to control his own physical reach, requiring the capability to recognise and respond to messages from the muscles directing his arm movements. All of this was founded on an ability to focus on objects in his immediate environment and recognise their existence as separate from himself, a skill he had been practising from birth. The notion that babies have only short attention spans is also refuted as Jake persists in his task until he is successful; only once he can achieve it without difficulty does he loses interest and call out in search of further mental stimulation. Examined in this way, the seemingly simple activity of reaching out for the basket handle can be recognised as extraordinarily complex, entirely self-motivated learning.

Neuroscience research shows that all learning depends on neural networks distributed across many regions of the brain, such as the motor cortex, sensory cortices and language areas. Jake's achievement supported the connection of neurons (brain cells) in relation to motor and sensory development so it is evident that the wider the range of types of experience, the deeper and more secure will be the learning. This is referred to as multi-sensory learning and is a crucial factor in children's development.

Inductive learning

An ability present from birth – and continuing throughout life, although we are largely unconscious of it – is a process known as statistical or inductive learning. This is the way young children identify patterns and regularities in the stream of their experience – for instance, knowing that food follows being seated in a high chair enables a hungry baby to stop crying and direct attention to other things because they recognise a meal is on its way. Inductive learning underpins how visual and auditory systems adapt as a result of experiences and so is fundamental to a large proportion of learning. Recognising patterns in speech – such as recurring syllables and sounds – accounts for how young children learn language with such rapidity and ease. Similarly inductive learning explains how young children form concepts and detect categories and how they are able to understand causal relationships between events.

Inductive learning is investigated by studying perceptual and cognitive capabilities of infants through habituation and dishabituation techniques (to become habituated to something is to grow used to it as it becomes familiar). When babies are first presented with a visual stimulus, they tend to stare at it and will move their head and eyes in order to locate it. After a period of time, the baby becomes used to looking at that particular stimulus (habituated to it) and so is likely to stop this looking behaviour. When a change is introduced to the stimulus, or a new stimulus is introduced, the looking behaviour returns. Through such habituation procedures, it is evident that babies as young as two months old can learn complex sequence patterns in a series of shapes. Once familiar with a pattern they show a preference for new patterns made up of the same shapes but shown in a different sequence (Kirkham et al. 2002). Adult caregivers can cater to this interest by creating simple visual patterns (such as one of those illustrated in Figure 2.1) at the end of a baby's cot – a sequence of simple shapes, changed from time to time to prevent over-familiarity, actively engages a baby's desire for perceptual stimulation at a stage when they are too young to be able to satisfy this for themselves.

Babies not only respond to visual sequences, but also pay great attention to patterns of sound heard around them. Like visual patterns, sounds do not just occur in fixed sequences, but nor are they completely random – there are 'transitional probabilities' of one sound 'shape' following another. Babies are able to detect auditory similarities and differences very early in life. Kuhl (2004) has shown that

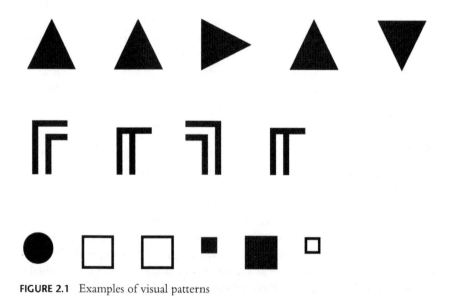

FIGURE 2.1 Examples of visual patterns

infants' brains track statistical dependencies and identify conditional probabilities between sound elements, using this perceptual information to construct proto-type patterns of sounds. Adults instinctively take this into account and adjust their language when talking with babies, speaking in a simpler register with frequent repetition to make it easier for them to pick out specific sounds. The process is further reinforced when adults echo infants' early attempts to vocalise, highlighting how much perceptual learning depends upon social interaction. It is only in the context of joint interactions with caregivers that babies can apply statistical learning of sound patterns; they do not learn language from watching video images or tele-vision (Kuhl et al. 2003). Active and meaningful experiences are necessary so that memory becomes embedded.

Learning by imitation

Young children are also proficient from a very early age at learning through imita-tion. A striking example of this is how babies actively copy face and hand gestures at only a few days old. As with the example of Jake reaching for the handle of his basket earlier in the chapter, it is easy to underestimate the physical and neural processes involved in such seemingly straightforward behaviour. For a very young baby to be able to observe an adult perform an action like putting out their tongue, recognise the equivalent parts of their own body and manage their own immature motor cortex to perform the same action shows a level of cortical organisation from birth not recognised until very recently. Evidence suggests this is accom-plished by what is termed the 'mirror neuron' system, meaning that the same neu-rons fire when another person is observed performing a particular action as when the action is performed by the self.

Imitation becomes more complex as babies develop so that by about nine months babies can learn to manipulate new objects by watching somebody else. This makes activity toys with buttons to press or buzzers that make a noise particu-larly enticing as well as, most importantly, the presence of others whose actions can be observed. Meltzoff (1995) showed that infants can also imitate *intended* actions; when an adult deliberately 'missed' putting a string of beads into a container, the baby was able to take the beads and put them in successfully, showing recognition of what the adult had intended. The significance of this is that not only does the mir-ror neuron system underpin imitation, but it also supports empathetic responses to other people's emotional states. By helping to understand the intentions of others and the recognition that other people are 'like me', infants' developing understand-ing of other minds is reinforced.

Imitation becomes increasingly valuable as a learning tool as children develop capacity for 'deferred imitation' (Bingham and Whitebread 2012: section 2.1). This means infants not only copy behaviour currently in front of them, but also reproduce the same behaviour on a later occasion, an achievement that depends on being able to mentally represent objects and events in the memory. This abil-ity is present from a surprisingly young age and develops rapidly; when shown a new toy, children from nine months old have been observed up to 24 hours later imitating actions they had previously watched. By 18 months the ability to do this has extended to two weeks and by two years of age children are capable of showing deferred imitation after delays of up to four months. These findings show how children's representational powers and ability to hold mental representations in long-term memory develop.

Learning by analogy

> Amir, 13 months old, is playing with a set of wooden blocks. He successfully places one on top of another and then a third on top of that. The next block is larger than the one beneath it and the structure collapses. He makes several attempts becoming increasingly upset. Jill, noting his frustration, shows Amir how, by placing smaller bricks on top, he can help his tower to balance. A few days later Jill observes Amir with a set of stacking beakers that, despite requiring a more complex technique, he eventually manages to successfully pile on top of each other in order of size.

Once children can actively construct patterns from experience through the processes described, they can start to apply these to make sense of new experiences or new information in different contexts. This is known as learning by analogy and refers to the capacity to notice similarities between one situation and another and transfer learning accordingly. An ability to generalise like this explains how children adapt to novel situations and start to tackle new challenges and problems. Amir does this with the stacking beakers as he is able to transfer his learning about putting smaller things on top of larger ones, learned in connection with blocks, when he comes across a new situation of stacking beakers. Various studies demonstrate infants' ability to make use of strings, boxes, different tools and other devices to solve problems and achieve a desired outcome, such as reaching for an object beyond their reach. Such experiments show that young toddlers follow the same learning processes as older children, trying out different strategies to solve problems in increasingly sophisticated ways as they gain experience. Of course younger children's more limited knowledge may sometimes cause them to work from incorrect assumptions based on superficial features. For instance, I have observed toddlers, watching their mothers disappear towards the gate after being dropped off at nursery, using their thumb and forefinger on the glass in an attempt to enlarge the 'image'. They were trying to apply a technique relevant to tablets and digital pictures when the analogy does not apply in the real world of glass windows. Nonetheless, it is evident that infants are active learners able to incorporate learning from other situations to solve problems when they come across novel situations. Whilst research investigating learning by analogy has largely taken place in artificial laboratory circumstances, anybody spending time watching toddlers play will note many examples of this type of behaviour as children manipulate and experiment with objects. This highlights the value of plenty of open-ended equipment to encourage manipulation and experimentation as well as the importance of adults playing alongside children to support their investigations. In addition, recognising infants' tendency to climb on objects to reach for something outside their grasp as problem-solving behaviour can also change how adults respond to such strategies!

Acquisition of knowledge

Children's development and learning is highly dependent on the environment they experience. Since we all have different experiences, each child is individual and different from the next. The human brain is uniquely prepared to learn from early experience. While the brains of our closest animal relatives are already largely formed at birth (for instance the brain of a new-born chimpanzee is four-fifths of its full size), human brains grow around four times the size in the first five to six years of life. During this period massive growth in connections between neurons in the cerebral cortex occurs and these connections, or synapses, arise from children's early experiences; infants' brains are extremely plastic, meaning that connections grow and adapt in response to what they encounter. It is important though that awareness of this extraordinary growth does not lead to hyper-anxiety and over-reaction – Nutbrown and Page warn that 'images of the brain and talk of young brains atrophying due to lack of stimulation can strike fear into parents and practitioners alike. . . . Neuroscience can offer us something but . . . it is not the Holy Grail' (2008: 19–20).

At all ages, development is best supported by a strong focus on sensitive and responsive interaction. Underestimating infants' cognitive capabilities can result in a limiting regime that may meet their physical needs but restricts their ability to experiment and learn from their surroundings. This is a danger with formal readiness programmes that can narrow experiences to fulfil adult agendas instead of fostering young children's drive to extend their capabilities. Manipulative toys, heuristic play and loose parts equipment are particularity valuable in supporting infants' exploration of how things in the world around them function. By three months, babies are already forming ideas of how objects behave, looking longer at things that counter their expectations. Infants need lots of opportunity for independent exploration to test ideas and extend their learning. If Amir (above) simply watched Jill stacking bricks, she would do so in such a way that they naturally balanced; active experience is needed for learning by trial and error (Baillargeon 2004).

In the first years of life, sensory-motor experiences, movement and physical interaction in the world around them are all critical aspects of children's knowledge construction. Knowledge gained through interaction with the environment is enhanced through language, play and sensitive interaction, accumulating into 'cognition'. Information about the structure and action of physical objects and systems stems from children's perceptions of objects and events, such as how a thing behaves if it is pushed or dropped (naïve physics) or from their observations that some entities can change shape, colour or form and act by themselves (naïve biology). For instance birds fly and so do butterflies but cats and spiders don't. Similarly, children's experience of the mental states of others – the baby cries when she drops her toy – leads to a naïve understanding of psychology. Young children's learning goes beyond mere perception however as they try to construct causal explanatory frameworks about these physical, biological and psychological systems, searching for features that make category members similar or different. In this way a young child's early identification of all four-legged furry animals as 'dogs' is an understandable category error. Working from limited experience, it is an assumption that shows an ability to discriminate (in this case, between 'animals' and 'not animals') that will be refined as they gain more knowledge. Language enhances this process as the power to label things supports children's growing ability to categorise more accurately – for instance blackbirds, parrots and penguins are all different instances of birds.

As children interact with the environment in their daily lives, they become aware of dynamic inter-relations between people and objects around them. They try to make sense through constructing causal explanatory frameworks about the structure and action of things they perceive. An intrinsic desire to understand their environment, to be in active control of their own experiences, and to make relationships with other children and adults leads to accumulation of knowledge about the causes and effects of what is perceived around them. This forms the basis of their cognition – simple knowledge in the domains of physics, psychology and biology that will develop into more complex concepts as they mature.

> Megan (3½) is playing in the water tray with a variety of objects provided to support concepts of floating and sinking. She discovers that a ping pong ball, a paper boat and pieces of polystyrene that the children have been using as 'snow' for a Christmas scene will all float, whilst a wooden block, a toy car and a spoon do not. She decides that things float 'because they are white' and explains her theory to Nicky, her keyworker. Nicky searches in the outdoor equipment cupboard for a golf ball and offers it to Megan to test her idea – 'I wonder what will happen if you try this?' she suggests.

Megan's partial understanding of physical processes can be seen in her simplistic deduction that the colour of objects is what makes them float. Although naïve, this is not a random or illogical idea; speculating from the evidence of her own experiment she has identified what all the floating objects have in common. Restricted experience has prevented her from reaching a more informed conclusion and so Nicky, rather than correct her mistake, offers Megan a new object that will challenge the hypothesis and encourage her to revise her ideas. In this way, young children's fundamental assumptions about the structure of their world, how things work and the underlying nature of its categories are crucially dependent on their experience.

Cognitive control processes

A number of cognitive control functions are needed for concentration, for thinking and for controlling initial impulses. These are called *executive functions* and include cognitive flexibility, inhibition (in other words, self-control and deliberate mastery of one's own behaviour), and working memory. Development of these fundamental aspects of cognitive growth underpins children's ability to problem-solve, reason and plan, forming the foundation for development of higher cognitive processes well into adulthood. It used to be assumed that these abilities only developed during adolescence but it is now recognised that these functions, of particular importance when encountering a new problem, emerge towards the end of the first year and continue to develop during infancy and the preschool period. This happens in two stages – the skills underlying executive function emerge in the first years of life and then from three years of age, basic skills become integrated and coordinated (Garon et al. 2008). Five components make up the executive functions and contain both cognitive and affective, or emotional, elements – these are inhibitory control, working memory, internalised speech, motivational appraisal and behavioural appraisal (Bingham and Whitebread 2012: section 2.1).

- Inhibitory control refers to children's capacity to actively control their impulses and overcome impetuous or inappropriate behaviour. Resisting immediate impulse requires children to be able to manage internal conflict, developing self-regulation. Ability to do these things improves with age.
- Working memory is the system by which information is held in mind, ready to call on to perform cognitive tasks such as reasoning or comprehension. Because there are visual- and sound-based working memory systems, this is particularly important for learning to read as well as metacognition – a concept explored later in this chapter. Although various factors affect the volume of material stored in the working memory, capacity increases with age.
- Internalised speech is the way children guide their actions by thinking out loud. Whilst young children use this form of self-talk to consciously focus on tasks even in the company of others, it gradually tapers off, becoming internalised as thought.
- Motivational appraisal refers to how emotions and motivation affect cognitive processes and the way that performance is affected by children's level of interest and the personal relevance of an activity. Children's emotional response, for instance their level of confidence, if they struggle and find a task difficult, as well as reasons they attribute to previous success or failure on similar tasks, all have an effect.
- Behavioural appraisal concerns ability to recognise and thereby exert a measure of control over one's own behaviour. This self-regulation is an important aspect of social competence.

Each of these different executive functions develops alongside each other in the preschool years as the frontal lobe cortex matures (Diamond 2013). It is important to remember that development and learning processes involve both cognitive and emotional aspects. Children's interest and engagement, their feelings of competence, autonomy and relatedness through positive social relationships, all impact on development and ability to self-regulate. These research findings redefine the concept of learning. A view of children needing to be taught in order to learn and develop is clearly incompatible with what is known of infants' innate systems for self-regulation maturing over time within appropriate contexts. The nature of these contexts and how they support children's learning are explored Chapter 3.

The importance of social interaction

> It is lunchtime and Jasmine (seven months) is sitting in a high chair with a bowl of rice and vegetables. She has a spoon in her hand and, although not yet able to successfully convey food to her mouth, her actions show that she understands its purpose. Meanwhile Mum feeds her, keeping up a running commentary throughout – 'Is that nice? You're enjoying your dinner, aren't you! Look, Mummy's got a spoon and Jasmine's got a spoon too – what a clever girl!' After a while Jasmine seems to be losing interest; her attention wanders and she looks intently at the fruit bowl on the table. Mum laughs – 'Oh, you want a banana, do you? Just one more spoon of rice first and then you can have some banana'.

The learning processes outlined in the first part of this chapter demonstrate the crucial importance of social interaction for young children's development. Vygotsky (1978) proposed a model of learning whereby development, driven by the child's curiosity, comes about through exploration and interaction within a social frame-work. Known as social constructivism, this recognises that children actively construct their own knowledge within a social context. Vygotsky suggested that all learning comes about initially at an *inter-mental* level (i.e. shared amongst others), as a result of experiences of joint attention expressed through spoken language. This can be seen in the episode above where the mother verbalises her child's experiences by com-menting on what is going on. She observes Jasmine looking at the banana, acknowl-edging the child's interest; this response gives significance to the act and values the baby's social communication. In time, learning becomes *intra-mental*, in other words it happens within the child's own mind in the form of internal language or thought. Vygotsky argued that development, or progress, comes about as children face chal-lenging tasks or problems. On their own they could operate at their level of actual development but with support from an adult or more able peer, they can achieve at a higher level (described as their 'level of potential or proximal development').

Infants demonstrate very early predisposition and ability to interact with others. This is matched by a powerful tendency in adults to interact with, and read mean-ing into, the behaviours, actions and vocalisations of babies. Trevarthen and Aiken (2001) have documented these tendencies over many years, producing detailed video analysis of mother and child interactions. These reveal what Trevarthen char-acterises as 'proto-conversations' and establish the early emergence of children's ability to derive meaning through interaction and inter-subjectivity.

A key element of early communicative episodes is creation of mutual attention as seen in Jasmine and her mother's focus on the banana. This develops within the first two years of life as a growing child develops capacity for shared attention – the ability to jointly attend, with an adult, to an external object or event. It is most evident in the initial emergence of the pointing gesture – if Jasmine had been a little older she would have been able to point to the banana to make her intention clear. By 10 to 12 months, infants typically point to objects of interest that are out of reach and, shortly afterwards, they learn to locate objects pointed out to them by others (Tomasello et al. 2007). During their second year, children develop the ability to establish joint attention by following an adult's gaze. Again, the predisposition of adults to support this development, by closely monitoring the infant's gaze, looking in the direction of their gaze and using this focus of attention as the basis for further interaction (for instance by naming the object, commenting upon it or obtaining it for the child) has been documented in detail (Butterworth 2003). This is what Jasmine's mother does when she recognises the child's attention has wandered from her dinner, notices what she is looking at and says she can have some banana in a minute. Extensive studies of these adult–child interactions show that while there is a general tendency to support infants' early attempts to communicate, adults' sensitivity and styles of communication vary widely and these variations are clearly associated with differences in how children go on to learn, particularly in relation to how they learn language (Mundy and Sigman 2006).

The role of language

Children acquire phonological skills (knowledge of speech sounds that make up the fundamental components of language) throughout their toddler years by processes of statistical or inductive learning described earlier in the chapter. Motivating and stimulating social interactions are clearly crucial to this. Seeking to make sense of everyday life, young children encounter words being linked to perceptual experiences of events, objects and actions by carers who talk to babies before they can talk back, name the objects that are being used and comment on the child's behaviour and shared activities. In this way words initially feature as conceptual representations and precede language development (for instance, Jasmine would be able to recognise the words *spoon, banana, Jasmine* and *Mummy* long before attempting to say them). Knowledge of words is important for cognitive development because they constitute symbols; a word represents an object or an action but it is not the object or the event itself. Another form of symbol is gesture and the appearance of gesture is significant in language acquisition because it creates a bridge for children from non-verbal communication to speech and between comprehension of words and their actual production (Garber and Goldin-Meadow 2002). Gesture is used to express meaning before infants are able to produce language and shows the child's understanding of action symbols. Again, adults' support and their responses play a large part in this, for instance most infants will be encouraged to 'wave bye-bye' and the evident pleasure in this exchange that adults exhibit reinforces the child's desire to communicate.

Language development entails both learning vocabulary and acquisition of grammar, although the latter is unconscious – indeed many adults, even those with good mastery of spoken and written language, have only a hazy idea of how grammar 'works'. Vocabulary development increases exponentially in early childhood and around the age of two children develop the capacity to absorb new words very quickly, learning about ten new words a day. The developmental range varies greatly between individual children depending on experiences and environment but the median English spoken vocabulary at age 16 months is 55 words. By 23 months this has increased to 225 words, rising to 573 words at 30 months. By the age of six years the median measure (that is, the midpoint of frequency measures) for spoken vocabulary is 6,000 words and comprehension vocabulary is around 14,000 words; comprehension vocabulary continues to exceed expressed vocabulary throughout life. Different phonetic systems and consonant/vowel structures affect acquisition of vocabulary so these figures may differ for other languages although the general pattern of growth remains the same. Research across different language speakers indicates that young children's language development follows the same trajectory (Waxman and Goswami 2012). Bilingual or multilingual children are likely to take a little longer in producing words because they are processing two languages (or more) alongside each other. Once they begin to speak they rapidly catch up though and accessing two different symbolic systems benefits children in terms of increased cognitive flexibility.

Children learn new vocabulary through a combination of the context in which words are encountered alongside their position in a sentence helping to eliminate alternative meanings.

> On a walk to the park to feed the ducks, Millie (22 months) is distracted by the sight of a bald man – something she has never encountered before. Turning to her father with a look of puzzlement she tells him 'Man . . . hair . . . uhoh!' Her father laughs – 'Yes, he's bald isn't he? Have you ever seen a bald man before?'

This example demonstrates how, when a child lacks the correct word, sensitive adults will gently feed it to them – although Millie shows how creative children can be in expressing themselves effectively even with limited vocabulary! On this occasion, Dad saying that the man is 'bald' and then again referring to him as 'a bald man' reinforces the meaning of the word and provides a context in which to use it. From a grammatical point of view this establishes 'bald' as an adjective we can use to describe certain people. Although Millie's father does not intend to give a lesson in grammar, the language template that he provides supports his daughter's development in both vocabulary and grammar.

Once children have a small vocabulary of useful words they begin to put two words together ('More juice?' 'Daddy come!') followed by three word sentences. Although these utterances may seem ungrammatical on the surface, this is far from true. Rather than being random strings of words, the structure of infants' sentences follows the grammatical patterns they hear around them – for instance whilst a child may make comments along the same lines as 'Daddy come' (such as 'Mummy come!', 'Daddy gone!' or 'Milk gone!'), it is noticeable that they will not reverse the order of words to say 'come Mummy' or 'gone milk'. Millie's sentence is more complex – though it lacks a verb, she nonetheless demonstrates understanding that the subject (in this case 'man'), must come before the object (his hair) and that a sentence may include an additional clause to provide more information (uhoh!). Observation of such natural and unconscious use of syntax led Chomsky (1965) to speculate that language is innate, stemming from a 'Language Acquisition Device' located within the human brain. In recent years this has been challenged and Tomasello et al. (2005) argue that the process of language acquisition is inherently social, taking the form of cultural learning. Children randomly encounter appropriate linguistic forms in the course of everyday life, gradually building on these piecemeal constructions using the same pattern-finding mechanisms that underpin learning in other domains, such as statistical learning, categorisation, induction and analogy. As with other forms of learning, social interaction is crucial in supporting and encouraging this process and adults give children feedback on incorrect use of language, not by explicit correction but by reformulating what they say. For instance, inductive learning would lead a young child to assume that all past tenses end in the suffix *ed* whereas the English language contains a considerable number of irregular verbs. Rather than telling the child they are wrong, adults can model the correct form in their response.

> I runned very fast, didn't I?
> Yes you did – you ran really fast!

The relationship between language and higher-level cognitive abilities

Vygotsky (1986) detailed several ways that language progressively becomes a way of self-regulating action and thought during the early years. The ability to refer backwards into memory and project forwards in time develops through language, alongside children's increasing capacity to represent thought mentally in the form of words. Being able to vocalise thought enables children to separate out the emotions experienced during an event from their cognitive understanding of its factual content. This means, for instance, that they can explain how they were sad when their friend didn't want to play with them and thereby understand what happened as well as to process their feelings and work out a strategy to make up with their friend.

At first infants are totally dependent upon caregivers to label objects and experiences verbally and to provide syntax until they build up a bank of vocabulary and verbal expressions. As children begin to talk, self-speech (or private speech) features heavily in their mental self-regulation until a point around five or six years old when words spoken aloud become internalised into a stream of con-sciousness. Self-talk enables a child to sustain attention and guide themselves through activities; indeed many adults revert to talking out loud when they need to concentrate or tackle a tricky task. When more experienced others verbally explain reasons and strategies to children (e.g. *I think Jamie's sad because he wanted a ride on the bike too. Perhaps you could be kind and give him a turn soon*), children are able to acquire self-language, or private speech, that they can use as a technique for controlling action and thought and to understand their own motivations and behaviour.

In this way language supports cognitive processes as executive function skills and working memory capacity contribute to reasoning. Having verbal labels allows children to keep two things in mind at once and being able to remember verbal instructions enables them to stay on track. Language also assists young children's developing capacity to reflect and plan by supporting mental consideration of alternatives before they take action. As an aid to memory, language helps children remember things that have happened and relate them to new intentions, using learning from past experience for future occasions and to form new concepts, ideas and solutions to problems. There appears to be a high correlation between verbal ability and young children's cognitive flexibility and complex working mem-ory which supports the notion that language and control processes are associated (Bingham and Whitebread 2012: section 2.1). This highlights the importance of language, beyond communication and literacy, as a tool for higher-level thinking skills that are fundamental to lifelong processes of learning.

Development of a Theory of Mind

> Poppy and Jack (21 and 22 months old) sit alongside each other playing with Sticklebricks. Jack has successfully stuck quite a number together and Poppy watches him with interest. She is attempting to do the same when she catches sight of a plate from the role play area lying nearby. Retrieving the plate, she arranges several separate Sticklebricks on it then picks one up and pretends to eat it. Jack sees her and giggles so Poppy puts the plate between them where they can both reach it. Jack fetches a teddy and taking one of the bricks proceeds to 'feed' him with it. 'Teddy biscuit' he tells Poppy.

Whilst children's development initially stems from sensorimotor activity, as we have seen, language subsequently plays a substantial part in enriching children's cognitive skills. After their first year, this is further enhanced by imaginary or pretend play. Both language and imaginative play share the core developmental functions of enabling children to reflect upon and regulate their own cognitive behaviour and gain deeper understanding of the mind. Imaginative play, particularly socio-dramatic play, enables children to do so through action and, during their second year, young children start to show signs of using their imagination through inventing pretend situations. Joining with others in imaginative scenarios enriches learning as they combine and build on each other's thinking. For instance, in the scene above, we do not know that Poppy intended the bricks to represent biscuits; they might have been cakes, carrot sticks or anything else in her imagination. Simulated biting however, made it evident that she was pretending they were something to eat. Jack's ability to 'read' the situation and recognise Poppy wasn't simply chewing on a brick as a younger infant might do, is evidence of his own understanding of pretence and he joins in by feeding teddy. This action and his labelling of the 'food' as 'biscuits' moves the play forward and between them the children create an imaginary scenario that exists in their joint minds.

Pretend play starts out simply, for instance an adult and baby pretending to drink from empty cups, but gradually begins to reveal more sophisticated signs of imagination in detaching the use of an object from its visual identity – for instance in using a stick or a banana as a gun. This is a sign of children's growing representational ability as they manipulate symbols, and indicates developing awareness of their cognition, seen in the ability to separate out aspects of their own knowledge. In order to pretend that an object is something else within the imaginary scenario, Poppy and Jack had to separate the primary representation of the object (the Sticklebrick: plastic, prickly and brightly coloured) from their imagined representation (something to eat). For this they needed to detach and override their knowledge of 'brickness' from 'biscuitness' so the emergence of imaginative play signifies the beginning of a capacity to understand items of knowledge, or thoughts, as entities in themselves.

Individual differences in children's preferences for pretend play and the types of conversation in which they engage are wide. For example children with siblings generally show earlier development of a theory of mind (i.e. an understanding that others have a mind like their own) than children with no brothers or sisters. One reason that pretend play with siblings and friends helps develop psychological understanding is that shared pretend play makes high demands for imaginary and cooperative interaction. Shared socio-dramatic play provides a large number of opportunities for reflecting upon one's own and others' desires, beliefs and emotions and high-quality pretend play has repeatedly been shown to be closely associated with the development of cognitive, social and academic abilities (Whitebread 2012). Interestingly, Lillard has shown (2002) that as children get older less time is spent in actual role play, and more and more time is spent in negotiating the plot and each other's roles.

Socio-dramatic play places particular demands on children's self-restraint and the ability to self-regulate as it obliges children to follow social rules. In the example of Poppy and Jack, this was a simple representation of eating biscuits – an activity familiar to most toddlers and straightforward to enact. The ability to pretend is a complex cognitive skill however and develops gradually through interaction with others. Adults are able to support this development by acting as a bridge between the real and the imaginary, using the language of pretend to support children's growing understanding. This is illustrated in the following extract from my research diary:

> Sarah (2.2) is playing on her own with the zoo. I sit close by and watch as she concentrates on sorting the different animals. She carefully selects all the tigers, showing no interest in any of the other animals which she leaves in a heap. She places the tigers in a line ordering them in size, then looks up and notices me watching. 'Tigers!' she says, and then 'Mummy tigers . . . baby tigers'. 'Yes, you've got lots of tigers, haven't you?' I agree. Sarah starts to walk her tigers around the mat until she has lined them all up beside me. She picks up the first one and makes 'pecking' motions on my leg with its mouth. She giggles and I say 'Ouch! That tiger bit me!' Sarah stops laughing at once and looks very serious – 'Sorry' she says. I immediately explain that I was only pretending, the tiger didn't really hurt me. I pick up another tiger and make the same motion on her leg. 'Look, the tiger's biting you now!' She starts to laugh and we take it in turns to bite each other with tigers.

This observation shows Sarah in the early stages of imaginary play as she animates the tigers, attributing roles (mummies and babies) to them and making them walk around the carpet. Although she herself initiates the biting action, her understanding of 'let's pretend' is still developing and so her reaction to my 'Ouch!' is located in the real world of the nursery rather than the imaginary scenario where tigers roam. It is only when she says 'Sorry' that I realise her misinterpretation of my response and hurry to reassure her that the tiger did not *really* hurt me, I was only pretending. Reversing the situation so that I pretended to bite Sarah with a tiger reinforced the idea. Adults' verbal explanations and active involvement can support young children in engaging in imaginative play as well as enabling greater understanding of others' roles and actions. Small world equipment is beneficial for this as well as role play and appropriate props such as dressing up clothes that enable children to take on and explore different ways of being. As children get older and engage in more complex scenarios they have to take into account the different roles, motivation, actions and attitudes of the characters they portray which makes high demands on their psychological understanding.

Theory of Mind (ToM) is attributed to children who are able to use knowledge of their own and others' mental states to understand others' behaviour. Between the ages of three and five years, an important transition in ToM conceptualisation occurs as children begin to understand that they themselves, as well as other people, can hold and act on false beliefs. Evidence suggests a purposeful relation between executive functions and ToM (Bingham and Whitebread 2012: section 2.1). Clear correlation has been established between verbal ability and ToM performance in both typically and atypically developing children.

Metacognition

Symbolic systems of language and imaginative play allow children to detach themselves from the immediate situation and therefore enable cognition itself to become the object of thought and reflection (Waxman and Goswami 2012). Both make a significant contribution to metacognition, the awareness of one's own thinking processes. Metacognition includes the ability to monitor the current state of one's knowledge or memory, or how well an activity or strategy is working to make adjustments to the cognitive strategies being used and improve performance. As higher level processing and control systems mature and children's processing skills become more sophisticated and efficient, they are increasingly capable of reflection on their own thinking processes. Astington and Baird-Smith (2005) suggest that talking about the mind focuses children's attention on explicit mental explanations of behaviour, introducing them to a vocabulary of terms for unseen and abstract concepts such as thoughts, feeling, ideas, memories and so forth that they cannot directly observe for themselves. This understanding begins to develop in early childhood; three- to four-year-olds are able to use simple verbs for mental operations correctly (e.g. knowing, learning, remembering), but more complex concepts (such as estimating, believing, predicting) are still difficult for children at age six (Schraw and Sinatra 2004). The development of conscious awareness of cognitive processing marks an important advance in cognitive control. Children can now learn to direct and monitor their learning, thinking and problem-solving activities more reliably and independently. They can become responsible for their own learning and thinking, as well as their behaviour, in significant ways that form the foundations for development as self-regulating learners.

Nelson and Narens' (1990) model of metacognitive processing suggests that when undertaking mental tasks, activity operates on at least two levels simultaneously. The intended activity takes place at *object* level, but at the same time, at *meta* level, the overall goal is held in mind so that stored information can be retrieved from long-term memory. For example a child attempting to fit a shape into a puzzle (object level) can draw on previous experiences with other puzzles and fitting toys (meta level) to help figure out a solution. By continually checking progress at meta level they can make adjustments at object level if necessary. Information flowing in both directions helps children continuously adjust their strategies, creating a feedback loop that results in more efficient performance. Sometimes this processing is conscious, particularly when attempting new tasks, but metacognitive activity mostly happens without awareness.

Metacognitive capacities of young children are evident from observing strategies they use to correct mistakes when playing with manipulative items such as shape sorting boxes and simple fitting toys; this can be seen from as early as 18 months. The significance of an individual's ability to monitor and regulate their own cognition and to develop increasingly sophisticated metacognitive knowledge of their capabilities is particularly relevant to later education – for instance, reasoning and problem-solving, mathematics, reading and text comprehension – and it has been established that children with learning difficulties commonly exhibit metacognitive deficits.

Self-regulation

Self-regulation refers to fundamental aspects of emotional, social, cognitive and motivational development and is the basis for development of a wide range of skills and dispositions strongly associated with children becoming successful learners and socially adept adults. Within the early years of life, increasing self-awareness leads to more and more control of children's own mental processing such as thinking, reasoning and remembering. These are processes that underpin the whole range of development, including emotional and social abilities.

Self-regulation integrates emotional and cognitive aspects. Development of metacognitive, self-regulatory executive functions have been related to developments in specific brain regions that may play a functional role in the deployment of attention and in processing and regulation of emotion, cognition and behaviour. Uttal (2011) however warns of too much emphasis on explaining psychological processes through a focus on brain activity, pointing out how the extraordinary plasticity of the brain means activity is widely distributed across all areas.

Children's self-regulatory and metacognitive abilities across cognitive, emotional, social and motivational domains emerge and develop from birth up to the end of primary school and make a unique contribution to learning performance beyond that accounted for by traditional measures of intelligence. Whilst Whitebread et al. (2009) have identified metacognitive and self-regulatory behaviours in children as young as three years engaged in playful activities, unsuitable provision that does not support the development of such skills has serious implications as will be considered in later chapters. Emotions such as enjoyment, hope, anxiety or boredom all affect learning; positive emotions support children's effort, interest and ability to self-regulate learning whereas negative emotions result in lack of interest, distraction and need for external regulation (Pekrun et al. 2002). The consequences of this go beyond the immediate situation, strongly affecting academic development and laying the foundations for later life success (Morrison 2015).

Conclusion

This chapter has examined the emergence, from birth onwards, of various cognitive processes that enable young children to learn about their environment by constructing ideas based on observation and experiences, imitating others' behaviours and making analogies by forming associations with previous knowledge. These are all effective processes for early learning and lead to the development of more sophisticated executive functions such as attention, working memory and inhibitory control supporting thinking and remembering. The evidence considered here has demonstrated that a child's brain has essentially the same structures and performs the same functions as adult brains, hence cognitive development is largely a matter of neural enrichment. Supportive environments in the home, school and wider culture enable experiential learning and lay the basis for the cognitive and emotional functioning of the adult system.

As the next chapter makes clear, learning does not take place within the brains of individual children but is dependent on social interaction within cultural contexts: adults, other children, resources and the environment are all important influences on development. Central to the whole process are relationships with others and the quality of early social interactions are crucial in laying appropriate foundations for further learning. In particular social interaction supports development of language as a symbolic and abstract system through which children make sense of their learning, share ideas and compare them with others. Children gradually become able to talk themselves through activity using private speech or self-direction commentary, eventually becoming fully self-regulating through use of internal speech or abstract thought. Vygotsky (1978) emphasised the importance of play for children to reach their zone of proximal development (ZPD) and active hands-on exploration and experience are essential factors in development. Whilst all areas of development are promoted by play, imagination in particular has important consequences for cognitive development. Through the channels of pretend play even very young children can think and reason about experiences and ideas in sophisticated ways.

An important aspect of development is the notion of self-regulation, or children's increasing capacity to regulate their cognition, emotions and behaviour. Conceptualising self-regulation as adaptive control emerging through infancy and early childhood and observable in emotional, behavioural and social processes as much as cognitive ones focuses the lens upon the powerful learning processes at work early in life. These enable mastery of basic skills in preparation for later, more sophisticated regulatory competencies.

Whilst evidence demonstrates that many of the metacognitive and self-regulatory skills can be explicitly encouraged in young children, it clearly refutes the notion that children need be prepared for learning – they have been actively and effectively engaging in learning from birth. This strongly challenges the readiness agenda with its associated assumptions of the need for formal instruction and academic content. On the contrary, evidence of young children's strong exploratory drive to make sense of their experiences suggests that they need opportunities that can actively engage their growing capabilities and understanding. These should take place within environments that are interactive and collaborative because young children's learning is social in origin. Interaction with sensitive and responsive adults and active engagement in reciprocal relationships with peers support their growing sense of self. Open-ended activities that offer possibilities for problem-solving, creativity and imagination can best foster the development of language, cognitive functioning and self-regulation – all traits that ready children for future school success. The danger is less that children will not be ready for school but rather that formal expectations of school have the potential to shut down and deny young children's competencies. The implications of this and the ways that children's natural drive towards learning and development lays the groundwork for more formal learning will be explored in next chapter.

References

Astington, J.W. and Baird-Smith, J. (2005) *Why language matters for theory of mind*, Oxford: Oxford University Press.

Baillargeon, R. (2004) The acquisition of physical knowledge in infancy: a summary in eight lessons, in U. Goswami (ed), *Blackwell handbook of child cognitive development*, Oxford: Blackwell.

Bingham, S. and Whitebread, D. (2012) *School readiness: a critical review of perspectives and evidence*. Report prepared for TACTYC, available at www.tactyc.org/projects. Accessed June 25, 2016.

Butterworth, G. (2003) Pointing is the royal road to language for babies, in S. Kita (ed), *Pointing: where language, culture, and cognition meet*, Mahwah, NJ: Erlbaum.

Central Advisory Council for Education (CACE) (1967) *Children and their primary schools* (The Plowden Report), London: HMSO.

Chomsky, N. (1965) *Syntactic structures*, The Hague: Mouton.

Diamond, A. (2013) Executive functions, *Annual Review of Psychology*, Vol 64: 135–68.

Garber, P. and Goldin-Meadow, S. (2002) Gesture offers insight into problem-solving in adults and children, *Cognitive Science*, Vol 26 (6): 817–831.

Garon, N., Bryson, S.E. and Smith, I.M. (2008) Executive function in preschoolers: a review using an integrative framework, *Psychological Bulletin*, Vol 134 (1): 31–60.

Goswami, U. (2015) *Children's cognitive development and learning*, York: Cambridge Primary Review Trust.

Kirkham, N.Z., Slemmer, J.A. and Johnson, S.P. (2002) Visual statistical learning in infancy: evidence for a domain general learning mechanism, *Cognition*, Vol 83: B35–B42.

Kuhl, P.K. (2004) Early language acquisition: cracking the speech code, *Nature Reviews Neuroscience*, Vol 5: 831–843.

Kuhl, P.K., Tsao, F.-M. and Liu, H.-M. (2003) Foreign language experience in infancy: effects of short-term exposure and social interaction on phonetic learning, *Proceedings of the National Academy of Sciences*, Vol 100: 9096–9101.

Lillard, A. (2002) Pretending, understanding pretence and understanding minds, in S. Reifel (ed), *Play and culture studies*, Norwood, MA: Ablex.

Meltzoff, A.N. (1995) Understanding the intentions of others: re-enactment of intended acts by 18-month-old children, *Developmental Psychology*, Vol 31: 838–850.

Morrison, F.J. (2015) Understanding growth in self-regulation: international contributions, *Early Education and Development*, Vol 26 (5–6): 893–897.

Mundy, P. and Sigman, M. (2006) Joint attention, social competence and developmental psychopathology, in D. Cicchetti and D. Cohen (eds), *Developmental psychopathology: theory and methods* (2nd ed), Hoboken, NJ: Wiley.

Nelson, T.O. and Narens, L. (1990) Metamemory: a theoretical framework and new findings, in G. Bower (ed), *The psychology of learning and motivation: advances in research and theory*, Vol 26, New York: Academic Press.

Nutbrown, C. and Page, J. (2008) *Working with babies and children from birth to three*, London: Sage.

Pekrun, R., Goetz, T., Titz, W. and Perry, R.P. (2002) Positive emotions in education, in E. Frydenberg (ed), *Beyond coping: meeting goals, visions, and challenges*, Oxford: Oxford University Press.

Schraw, G. and Sinatra, G.M. (2004) Epistemological development and its impact on cognition and academic domains, *Contemporary Educational Psychology*, Vol 29: 95–102.

Tomasello, M., Carpenter, M., Call, J., Behne, T. and Moll, H. (2005) Understanding and sharing intentions: the origins of cultural cognition, *Behavioural and Brain Sciences*, Vol 28: 675–735.

Tomasello, M., Carpenter, M. and Liszkowski, U. (2007) A new look at infant pointing, *Child Development*, Vol 78 (3): 705–722.

Trevarthen, C. and Aitken, K. (2001) Infant intersubjectivity: research, theory and clinical applications, *The Journal of Child Psychology and Psychiatry and Allied Disciplines*, Vol 42 (1): 3–48.

Uttal, W.R. (2011) *Mind and Brain: A critical appraisal of cognitive neuroscience*, Cambridge, MA: MIT Press.

Vygotsky, L. (1978) *Mind in Society*, Cambridge, MA: Harvard University Press.

Vygotsky, L. (1986) *Thought and Language*, Cambridge, MA: MIT Press.

Wastell, D. and White, S. (2012) Blinded by neuroscience: social policy, the family and the infant brain, *Families, Relationships and Societies*, Vol 1 (3): 397–414.

Waxman, S.R., and Goswami, U. (2012) Learning about language and literacy, in S. Pauen and M. Bornstein (eds), *Early childhood development and later achievement*, London: Cambridge University Press.

Whitebread, D. (2012) *Developmental psychology and early childhood education*, London: Sage.

Whitebread, D., Coltman, P., Pino Pasternak, D., Sangster, C., Grau, V., Bingham, S., Almeqdad, Q. and Demetriou, D. (2009) The development of two observational tools for assessing metacognition and self-regulated learning in young children, *Metacognition and Learning*, Vol 4 (1): 63–85.

3

APPROACHES TO EARLY YEARS LEARNING

Introduction

Organisation of early years provision has changed over time as decades of research evidence informs our knowledge of how young children learn. Traditional transmission views of learning that positioned children as passive recipients ready to be filled with teacher-directed knowledge were first challenged by Piaget's notions of active learning. Piaget drew attention to how children construct their own knowledge through direct hands-on experiences but has since been criticised for underestimating the importance of social interaction and language and for assuming children are not ready to learn until they reach certain developmental stages. Nowadays early educators are more influenced by social constructivism, recognising that learning drives development and that all learning is social in origin. This position is outlined in Chapter 2 where examples strongly refute the idea that learning is something young children must be prepared for. On the contrary, it is evident they are active and competent learners from birth. Therefore the task of educators, rather than teaching young children predetermined items of knowledge, should be to harness and build on children's natural drive to investigate, explore and understand for themselves. This is a quite different task to the narrow focus on ensuring all children reach an arbitrary standard of school readiness at five years of age.

Two considerations arise from this position, namely *what* learning opportunities are offered for young children (curriculum) as well as *how* they are offered (pedagogy). Research across different countries (OECD 2006) reveals two broad tendencies that can be summarised as a focus on curriculum and content or else a more pedagogical approach founded in the socio-constructivist tradition. The latter emphasises natural unfolding of children's cognitive, emotional, social and physical capabilities as opposed to the former approach where curriculum takes precedence and children are assessed against a predetermined set of standards. This chapter considers the relationship between curriculum and pedagogy and explores how these issues impact on children's readiness. Essential ingredients of an appropriate pedagogy for young children are outlined in relation to research about effective learning and the concept of readiness.

Approaches to curriculum

The need for some degree of structuring and orientation of children's experiences in the form of a curriculum is widely accepted and most countries have documents in place to guide early childhood services. The age ranges covered vary, sometimes not beginning until age three (e.g. France, Portugal and Scotland) although earlier starting points are increasingly evident, such as the English *Early Years Foundation Stage* and Australian *Early Years Learning Framework* that both start from babyhood. Curricula usually stipulate a combination of academic areas and socio-emotional development (Wall et al. 2015) with areas of knowledge likely to include language and emergent literacy; numeracy; scientific concepts and reasoning; nature and the environment and general knowledge. Despite many similarities in content, there is significant variation in the way different countries implement their curriculum guidance. Countries taking a social pedagogic approach interpret curriculum documents as general guidance and provision tends to be play-oriented, employing children's own learning strategies. By contrast, when the focus is on preparing children for formal education, curriculum frameworks emphasise learning goals and child outcomes, and so become policy instruments aimed at promoting predefined standards for children's entry into primary school.

Countries with a tradition of social pedagogy, such as Scandinavia and many Central European countries, focus on the child as a whole person so place equal value on care, upbringing and learning. Early years establishments exercise a high degree of autonomy in determining their own curricula and, because the importance of each child's immediate social context is recognised, this happens in collaboration with parents and community. A holistic approach to learning is evident with emphasis on overall development rather than preparation (or 'readiness') for school and this way of working supports physical development, behaviour and self-regulation, communication skills and social competence as much as emergent literacy and numeracy. Children learn about basic science, numbers and literacy through real-life experiences and naturally occurring activities rather than by contrived sessions with predetermined subject content. They acquire knowledge naturally through making sense of their own experiences and increase in confidence as learners, making children ready for further learning challenges within primary school.

Children's ability to develop their own working theories through interaction with the physical and social environment is also prioritised in *Te Whāriki*, the early childhood curriculum of New Zealand. Rather than being subject-oriented, this is a philosophy-based approach that envisages curriculum as a mat (*whāriki*) interweaving principles (relationships; family and community; holistic development; empowerment) with strands (well-being, belonging, contribution, communication and exploration). Indigenous Maori culture is recognised in bi-cultural documentation with strong emphasis on services being responsive to changing needs of children and families. The distinctiveness of *Te Whāriki* builds on local values, rejecting universal concepts of child development and stressing diversity. Educators work closely with families who are involved in provision and contribute to assessment through *learning stories*, as do children themselves. Learning stories focus on children's dispositions towards learning rather than what they can or cannot do in readiness because children's developing sense of self is considered more important than school-based knowledge and process is valued over content.

Similar absence of predefined outcomes is evident in Reggio Emilia schools in Northern Italy. These take a localised, learner-centred approach rather than adhering to a centralised, uniform curriculum or any concept of children being ready to learn. Children are considered as social beings and active citizens with rights, so a 'pedagogy of listening' (Rinaldi 2006) is adopted, respecting children's need for active meaning-making. Cognitive development is fostered through jointly constructing knowledge and building up increasingly complex understandings of chosen themes. Within Reggio schools, the role of the educator is as co-learner, guiding, facilitating and researching alongside children who work together in collaborative project work.

These examples illustrate the way that curriculum frameworks reflect governments' perceptions of the purpose of early childhood provision and whether it is regarded as an important stage in its own right for young children as active citizens, or merely preparation (readiness) for what is to come later. The notion of ECEC as a preparatory stage results in early formalisation of numeracy and literacy ready for the demands of the first year in school. Yet it is evident that what young children are offered in the way of learning opportunities need not be a prescribed set of outcomes but may instead focus on their interests and experiences to encourage positive dispositions towards learning and development of critical thinking abilities. This process of learning is regarded as pedagogy, a broader concept than curriculum and one that draws on established theories of learning and development, including those of Piaget, Vygotsky, Bruner and Dewey, to encompass physical, emotional and social environments of young children.

In its attempts to raise standards the English government has encouraged the introduction of formal curricula at ever-earlier points in school. It has imposed a systematic programme for phonics teaching for example and continues to emphasise 'delivery' of literacy and numeracy in Reception classes. But research evidence indicates that this 'earlier is better' approach is misguided and will not make a difference in the long term. In contrast to the focus on early, didactic instruction in some Reception classes and certainly within Key Stage 1, current research suggests that long-term well-being and success at school are best supported by development of executive functioning and self-regulation abilities alongside satisfaction of children's need for feelings of autonomy, competence and relatedness (McClelland and Wanless 2015).

Pedagogy

Although pedagogy is often closely related to a curriculum, it concerns the *how* of adult–child interactions, recognising learning as a process rather than a product. Reviewing pedagogy in effective early years settings, Siraj-Blatchford et al. (2002) identify it as the interactive process between teacher, learner and the learning environment. This acknowledges the importance of social contexts within which children learn so development is the outcome of opportunities provided by specific relationships and environments where children construct their own understandings. This socio-constructivist approach has emerged as the dominant explanation for human development and learning and forms the bedrock of pedagogy for children's early years within the UK as in many other countries (Bingham and Whitebread 2012: section 1.5). An holistic pedagogical approach values natural learning strategies of young children such as learning through activity, play, social interaction and individual investigation. This supports children in their current developmental tasks and interests and can be fine-tuned to individual needs within specific contexts. Drawing attention to the complex and diverse nature of pedagogy in supporting children to flourish as valued individuals within a range of different contexts, Murray (2015) suggests that it might perhaps be more appropriate to talk about early years *pedagogies*.

With social constructivist pedagogies the quality of adults' interactions is fundamental to children's learning, so the skills, qualities and professionalism that practitioners bring to their work are central to an effective pedagogical approach (Moyles et al. 2002). Dahlberg and Moss (2005) suggest pedagogy should support children's involvement and participation through active listening, reflecting, discussing and interpreting. This contrasts with:

- curriculum-focused approaches where content and *what* children learn is of prime importance so teachers are reduced to technicians who impart knowledge, or
- constructivist perspectives (inspired by Piaget) where adults provide stimulating resources and opportunities but their own interaction with children's active learning is downplayed.

A consequence of adults' relational centrality means pedagogical effectiveness is related to practitioners' own ability to reflect on and fully articulate their pedagogy (Moyles et al. 2002; Stephen 2010). Although the statutory framework of the EYFS has no mention of the word pedagogy, acknowledgement of important pedagogical aspects are evident in its overarching principles of the unique child, positive relationship, an enabling environment and recognition that children develop and learn in different ways and at different rates. The focus on school readiness undermines the principles of social constructivism however, so that principles underpinning the EYFS can be in tension with its goal-driven content unless the teacher has a strong understanding of pedagogy. The challenges this raises are discussed in Chapter 6.

Essential ingredients of a pedagogy for early childhood

Effective pedagogies are those that facilitate positive interactions by structuring environments and planning activities that fully engage children (Wall et al. 2015). Children's cognitive and academic skills flourish in an environment where they feel confident and their independence and curiosity is encouraged. In contrast to the focus on early, didactic instruction, current research into early emotional and cognitive development suggests that long-term well-being and success at school are most powerfully supported by children's development of executive functioning and self-regulation and the satisfaction of their need for feelings of autonomy, competence and relatedness. By combining this understanding of children's cognitive, metacognitive and motivational development with empirical evidence from research into characteristics of high quality preschool provision, it is possible to identify key ingredients of effective early years pedagogy.

Children need to interact with the environment

Development occurs through participation in social and cultural contexts that support children's own inquiry. Young children's learning is dependent on the type of environment they experience and this can actively encourage, or severely limit, the learning process and affect how competent they feel as individual learners. Children need opportunities to learn independently as they pursue their own lines of interest and talk, work and play together: this requires freedom of movement, especially in outdoor spaces. The importance of an enabling environment, as acknowledged in the EYFS, is so great that within Reggio Emilia settings the environment is considered as the 'third teacher'.

Sensory-motor learning is the foundation of young children's cognitive development: an environment responsive to children's needs must incorporate opportunities for movement and active learning so they can develop cognitive cause-and-effect frameworks about structure and mechanisms of objects and people encountered in the world. Research suggests that learning is stronger if children learn new information using a variety of senses as it is spread across a larger network of neurons connecting a greater number of different neural structures. Therefore it is evident that children's cognitive development cannot be isolated from other learning and is completely intrinsic to physical activity. The need to explore, understand and assimilate their environment underpins children's successful progress in academic terms. Unfortunately classroom environments become progressively more restrictive once children begin formal schooling. Key Stage 1 (KS1) classrooms can leave little room for children's individual differences and this affects opportunities for autonomy, competence, cognition and motivation. Environments should allow adequate scope and choice of activities so children can achieve their own personal goals and develop the self-regulation processes that will underpin their learning.

Children need to construct their own learning

Piaget said that 'every time we teach a child something, we keep him from inventing it himself' (1972: 27). In reaction against earlier behaviourist models that believed children only learnt what they were taught, Piaget's *constructivism* emphasised the importance of active engagement with the environment. He argued that attempting to instruct young children was inappropriate since it prevented them from discovering for themselves. Although contemporary thinking rejects this view of the teacher as passive observer and facilitator, it nonetheless acknowledges the underlying premise that children need to be active in their learning, rather than simply receptive.

> Jo, a Year 1 teacher, knows her class enjoy the story 'Aliens Love Underpants' and so has used this to support understanding of number bonds up to 10. She takes 10 pairs of pants into the classroom and, using the alien puppets the children call Ping and Zog, tells the class the aliens have 10 pairs of underpants between them. Each day she thinks out loud 'Ping has 4 pairs of pants today – I wonder how many are left for Zog?' The children work out all the combinations which Jo helps them to record. She makes a point of leaving the pants out in a basket so children can return to them in their play. They play guessing games together, delighted when they count up and find they are right and supporting each other to self-correct if they get the answer wrong.

Social constructivist pedagogy still emphasises the pivotal need for active involvement in learning but maintains that it is the social context that initiates children's construction of knowledge. Ten pairs of underpants are insufficient in themselves for children to grasp number bonds, but linked to their interest in aliens and with plentiful social interaction to support thinking processes, this activity enabled children to discover number bonds for themselves and so construct their own knowledge. Jo could have taken another approach and used the underpants to explicitly teach her class number bonds but such direct instruction only brings about superficial learning – whilst children may learn to chant correct answers, they have not necessarily mastered the material and taken ownership of the ideas and so cannot transfer the learning to other contexts. Active involvement is crucial because it is through discovering and reinventing things for themselves, and through making mistakes, that learning becomes fully embedded in children's understanding. This process does not occur in isolation but is driven by social context. Children's initial sensory-motor representations, gained from interaction with the physical environment, become augmented by knowledge gained through action, language, pretend play and interaction with other people. The inter-relatedness of children's social and cognitive processes is fundamental to pedagogy as these psychological tools bring together psychological functioning *within* the child.

Teachers scaffolding learning

The importance of social interaction for children's learning highlights the crucial role of the adult; indeed it is the quality of interaction (a markedly different concept to 'instruction') that determines effective pedagogy (Moyles et al. 2002). As Chapter 2 demonstrated, children have a strong predisposition towards social interaction with adults from infancy, characterised as 'proto-conversations' (Trevarthen and Aitken 2001) and 'mutual attention'. Adults support development by closely monitoring the infant's gaze, looking where they are looking and using this focus of attention as the basis for further interaction. Willingness on the part of adults to respond to young children's attention focus needs to be continued into the early years of schooling as it forms the basis of Vygotsky's model of ZPD and so has particular implications for pedagogy.

The teacher's role is not as an instructor transferring knowledge into the minds of children, but as a 'scaffolder' (a metaphor suggested by Bruner, 1977) supporting, encouraging and extending children's own active construction of meaning and understanding. This requires sensitivity and responsiveness within joint-attention episodes. An effective teacher engages children's interest, simplifies tasks if necessary, highlights critical features, models key processes or procedures and, perhaps most importantly, sensitively monitors children's success in order to withdraw support when they can proceed independently. This scaffolding is evident in the aliens' underpants episode – Jo engaged the children's attention through an activity she knew would interest them, first modelling calculations herself, then providing an environment that enabled children to work out number problems for themselves. By observing their play and monitoring children's responses she was able to identify who had a thorough grasp of the procedure and who needed more support and individual interaction to scaffold their learning.

Verbal support is insufficient for effective use of the ZPD and cooperative activity promoting children's acquisition, mastery and internalisation of new knowledge is necessary to optimise learning. Teachers need to co-construct learning in joint performance with children, thereby creating the zone of proximal development of a new mental process. Children's mastery and internalisation of material is supported until the adult can begin to stand back. Incremental scaffolding is essential because neural networks are not suddenly restructured by one learning experience but develop over time, meaning teachers need to present cumulative information in the optimal sequence for new learners (Goswami 2015). Studies of children of different ages engaged in a wide variety of tasks show that adult encouragement, emotional support and scaffolding lead to increased effort and more successful performance when children attempt challenging tasks on their own (Bingham and Whitebread 2012: section 2d; Neitzel and Stright 2003).

The importance of play in creating ZPDs

Every child is a unique being who brings a whole range of experiences, individual abilities and dispositions to the learning process. It necessarily follows that any assumption that young children can all be taught the same information at the same time and in the same format is misguided. If learning is to be effective and long lasting it must arise from opportunities that are sufficiently open-ended to allow children to approach them in their own terms and take from them what they need. The significance of play is that it enables learning to be matched to each child's own development. Children's learning is enhanced by both free play and guided play and each is important for cognitive development (Moyles 2010).

The development of many core brain functions, such as cognitive flexibility, inhibition and working memory, problem-solving capacity, reasoning and planning occurs naturally for most children within play situations. Likewise, play affords opportunities for socio-emotional development where skills such as turn-taking, sharing and negotiating are required and the more expert other may be a peer rather than an adult. Since children are highly motivated to play, teachers can create zones of proximal development that support learning by providing specific activities to encourage development of various competencies and cognitions via play.

Practitioners can become involved in play on different levels but children are only likely to engage in the most complex forms of play, involving risk-taking and facing challenges, when they feel emotionally safe and secure. Developing a close and supportive relationship with each child is crucial to understanding their next step and adults' sensitive and timely responses to children's interests are key to building this knowledge. Moreover, it is important that the relationship is built through different experiences within the setting because a range of opportunities optimises occasions for children to use their natural learning strategies and develop self-regulation. Adults can be important to children's play through acting as 'play agents' (Weldermariam 2014) but they should also be mindful of potential negative effects of interrupting play that can impede learning. In their eagerness to ensure children's learning, adults often hijack children's play and so break the threads of their thinking (Fisher 2016).

> A baby clinic has been created at one end of the Reception class. Cots and baskets with a range of baby dolls have been provided as well as various equipment such as weighing scales, a baby bath, towels and baby clothes. Leaflets, charts and clipboards help create a literate environment but the children are free to use the area how they choose. The teacher observes how different children use the resource and notices that Ben and Ellie, who both have a new baby at home, spend a lot of time in the area. They play together with their 'babies' and have conversations about different aspects of caring for a baby. Ben has always been very boisterous in his play but in taking on the role of a responsible father he manages to exercise considerable self-control and the teacher is surprised to see how co-operative he is in negotiating a turn with the buggy. Yannick, recently arrived in the UK from France, usually hangs back from interacting with other children but seems keen on using the scales. He weighs each doll, tells Ellie and Ben their weights and records this on a chart. He proudly shows the teacher, reciting the numbers in French and English; this is the first time she has seen him so animated and is pleased at how much the role play area encourages his social interaction.

Appropriate levels of scaffolding can sometimes occur simply through adults providing appropriate equipment and materials to inspire and support young children to engage in various types of play together, naturally facing challenges that arise. Indeed, in some situations, such as the baby clinic above, adults may need to acknowledge the effectiveness of peers scaffolding each other rather than becoming directly involved themselves. Studies of young children's perceptions of play in educational settings (Howard 2010) demonstrate how children perceive hidden messages conveyed by practitioners about the nature of play. Children develop quite different perceptions from adults in the settings about what constitutes play; they tended to categorise activities as 'play' or 'not play' based on factors such as the amount of choice available, where the activity was situated, whether activities were 'enjoyable' and whether an adult was present. Adult involvement in children's play is a complex role and if it is to be productive it requires considerable skill and sensitivity. Fundamental to any involvement is clear understanding of what children are learning through play and how the quality of their experiences can be enhanced or undermined by the presence of an adult. Moyles (2010) suggests this is something practitioners may struggle with so that, although recognising the importance of child-initiated activity, they often cannot articulate a clear rationale. The negative consequence of this is that child-initiated activity is not fully utilised through fear of 'not being seen to teach' (p. 4).

For some areas of learning, guided play may be appropriate and sensitive adult involvement can enhance children's active playfulness. Guided play within educational contexts is quite distinct from free play and is characterised by setting up structured play environments around general curricula goals with objects, toys and materials designed to stimulate children's natural curiosity, exploration and play. Teachers play alongside children, asking open-ended questions and suggesting ways to explore materials that young children might not consider by themselves, but learning is child-directed, not adult controlled and children are the active drivers of the activity. This mixture of goal-oriented experiences with whole-child learning meshes core curricula and playful pedagogy. Experimental studies examining the impact on learning conclude that learning through guided play is at least as good, and often better, than direct instruction in supporting children's vocabulary, early numeracy and literacy and acquisition of concepts such as shape and space (Hirsh-Pasek et al. 2009). Some form of guided play with scales and weights could be helpful to tap into Yannick's enthusiasm in the baby clinic for instance if the teacher followed his lead, avoiding the temptation to take over play and use it as an opportunity to 'teach'.

Socio-dramatic play

Open-ended imaginative play opportunities have the flexibility to match a range of children's needs as can be seen in Ben, Ellie and Yannick's involvement in the baby clinic. Chapter 2 outlined the important role of imaginary play in children's holistic development so it is evident that such play has significant pedagogical potential.

Numerous studies confirm links between pretend play and favourable literacy outcomes (Bingham and Whitebread 2012: section 2d) and it also forms the cultural foundations of maths (Worthington and van Oers 2016). Imaginary, or socio-dramatic play aids development of imagination and thinking skills and learning occurs through formation of mental representations shown in children's language, gesture and symbols. Within symbolic play, objects take on meanings in children's imagination, irrespective of their function as real objects and this enables children to manipulate cognitive understandings and differentiate between various mental representations. The capacity to hold different ideas together in the mind is part of metacognition – the awareness of thinking processes and the ability to think about thinking itself. Often children engage in a mental state dialogue during dramatic play so it provides a medium for reflecting on and knowing about their own thoughts and, as much of children's imaginary play is with peers, it also supports understanding of others' emotions, mental states and perspectives and promotes the development of empathy.

Language is important in socio-dramatic play and social partners can use language to help others understand imaginary situations, but language is also the primary vehicle for self-regulation. Joint pretend play helps children check impulses and manage behaviour because it requires them to recognise and adhere to rules aiding the development of self-regulation, particularly inhibition. Self-regulation is fundamental to academic success and research demonstrates how it is fostered through make-believe activities (Bingham and Whitebread 2012: section 2.4). Although socio-dramatic play, such as the baby clinic scenario described earlier, may on casual observation appear to be free play, Vygotsky did not regard it as such. He pointed out that it is precisely in pretend play situations that children, acting within a role, voluntarily put aside any innate desire to act impulsively (for instance seizing a wanted toy for themselves) in favour of rule-based behaviour. This is evident in Ben's ability to curb his usual boisterousness and negotiate turn-taking with the baby buggy; by taking on the role of 'Daddy', rather than 'Ben', he is able to curb his impulsive behaviour and act in a more appropriate way. Vygotsky termed this 'the paradox of pretence' (1978: 100) where children subordinate immediate desires to the rules of play because of their need to become accepted members of the play situation. Developing the ability to self-regulate will support Ben in coping with classroom expectations of more formal learning as he gets older.

The power of self-regulation and growth of metacognition make socio-dramatic play a key ingredient of pedagogy but adult involvement in children's pretence is complicated and requires careful thought. It is known for instance, that adult scaffolding of imaginative play with toddlers supports symbolic development (Bigelow et al. 2004). Young children show more advanced imagination when imitating the pretence of others, meaning adults can provide support through role play. At later stages, thinking, reasoning and understanding may all be enhanced by pretend play scaffolded by an adult; but at the same time it is important that a teacher's presence does not inhibit play and take it in an adult-determined direction.

Consider for instance the ways in which the baby clinic might be more or less effective if a teacher played alongside the children.

Language as a tool of thought

Pedagogy is critically dependent on high quality verbal interactions (Siraj-Blatchford et al. 2002). Supporting early language development is clearly important in itself if teachers are to help children become articulate adults. But beyond this, language is of prime importance to cognitive development as children progress from initial stages of needing guidance and support to being able to do things independently. There is marked variation in language skills among children in the early years and they enter school having been exposed to significantly different language experiences. As learning arises from social interaction, the way children are supported by an adult is crucial to their progress and how adults talk to children will influence their understanding, memory and motivation. Both quality and quantity of spoken language are important in supporting communication and, because young children's vocabularies may differ greatly, gesture also has a part to play. Language and gesture are symbolic so, by enabling children to detach themselves from the immediate situation, they support metacognition (Goswami 2015).

> Nick, a Reception class teacher, has brought his younger brother's gerbil, Jimmy, into school and the children enjoy watching him roll round the carpet in his plastic exercise ball. Aisha tells the teacher 'He can't get out' and, misunderstanding her meaning, Nick replies, 'That's right Aisha, he can't get out of the ball so he'll be safe'. Aisha shakes her head and repeats 'But he can't get out'.
>
> 'Do you mean you think Jimmy wants to get out? Maybe he feels trapped in there and would like to run around like you do in the playground?'
>
> Aisha nods her head.
>
> 'Well I wonder what we could do to help him then? Is there any way we could let Jimmy run around on his own but still keep him safe, so he doesn't get lost . . . and nobody treads on him by mistake?'
>
> 'Could put him in a box!' says Harley. 'My Dad did that when my kitten was tiny'.
>
> 'That's a good idea, isn't it Aisha? Why don't you and Harley look for a box that Jimmy could play in?' Nick suggests.
>
> The children return with a large cardboard box from the junk modelling corner, put Jimmy inside and watch him run round exploring.

After a while Nick asks 'I wonder if there's anything we could do to make the box more interesting for Jimmy?' Aisha suggests a tube for him to run through and goes to fetch one. She returns with two cardboard tubes and the children start arguing about which would be best. Nick reminds them of the crawling tube in the nursery class garden; he helps them think about Jimmy's size and the width of each tube, using lots of vocabulary like 'wide', 'narrow' and 'too tight'. They realise the longer tube is no good for their purpose but are disappointed that the other one is so short.

'I wonder if there's anything we can do about that? Maybe we could join two tubes together?' suggests Nick.

Harley experiments with glue but the tubes keep coming apart; Aisha tries rubber bands. Eventually Harley remembers a roll of glued paper strip he used when he'd been making a submarine and that works well.

He talks aloud to himself: 'This will do it . . . cut it there . . . need another piece . . . '

Nick keeps a conversation going as the children work, suggesting different strategies, giving feedback on their progress and generally putting the experience into words for them. Over the course of the week other children join in until 'Jimmy's adventure playground' has expanded over considerable space and includes a maze, a bridge and a variety of apparatus for climbing.

Language provides a tool for children to think about and memorise their experiences and so internalise learning. Here Nick amplifies the children's own language, elaborating in a conversational style that supports their understanding and makes sense of what is happening. Nick helps them create their own mental representations, for instance by pointing out why it is important that Jimmy has a safe place to run about and making links to their experiences of play. At the same time he provides them with a language model and extends their vocabulary so they too can articulate these concepts. Through the medium of language, adults convey ideas and actions by encouraging, asking appropriate questions, clarifying tasks, reminding children of goals, making suggestions, giving feedback and so on. As young children begin to understand the steps modelled and articulated by a sensitive teacher, they become able to talk themselves through tasks using self-commentary or 'private speech'. This is a crucial bridging mechanism between external 'social speech', produced in the context of social interaction with another person, and fully formed 'inner speech' used to structure and keep track of thoughts. Self-commentary, apparent as Harley concentrates on cutting paper strips, appears up to the age of seven or eight years, gradually fading as the capacity for inner speech is established (Winsler and Naglieri 2003). Children become progressively able to self-regulate through internal speech but poor language skills will hinder a child in controlling their thoughts, emotions and actions.

In order to build on prior knowledge in joint interactions with adults, children need to remember and articulate what they have already learned. When a teacher adopts a dialogic style they support children in making sense of aspects of experience that lead to more organised learning and memory. Sharing relevant vocabulary and encouraging children to discuss and explain their ideas, as Nick does with Aisha and Harley, is key to helping them develop thinking skills and construct their own understandings about the world. Opportunities for active engagement in processes of interpretation and transformation of new experiences are also crucial. Tasks and ideas are most valuable to children when linked to contexts that carry meaning for them (Donaldson 1978) as the gerbil's care does for Aisha and Harley. The Effective Provision of Pre-School Education (EPPE) report (Sylva et al. 2004), showed a key element in high quality provision for young children is the occurrence of episodes of 'sustained shared thinking'. This is joint thinking about a shared focus that continues between children and adults over a period of time and it shifts the pedagogical imperative from the environment onto teachers' skilful and sensitive intervention (Roberts-Holmes 2014). Developing an adventure playground for Jimmy provides such a focus and opportunity to extend the children's learning within a play-based context.

Supporting children's own motivation

Successful learning at all ages and levels of education is underpinned by learners' motivation and connected to the extent an activity seems interesting and personally relevant to them. Effective teachers encourage children's motivation by building on their natural inclination instead of relying on external sanctions and controls. They look for ways to build teaching activities around children's interests, sense of fun and challenge, competencies and own choices. In this way children want to join in rather than being pressured into compliance by adults' inflexible attitudes or warnings of negative consequences.

> Back in Jo's Year 1 class, the children come in one morning to discover that Henry, the class bear, who always takes part in registration, is nowhere to be found (Jo has earlier hidden him in the Forest School area). She tells the children that Henry has been kidnapped and the police are investigating but they haven't been able to find Henry yet and need the children to help. Jo has provided a range of resources including police helmets, magnifying glasses, notepads, clipboards and iPads. The children follow clues that Jo has already set up including muddy footprints, bits of leaf, acorns and pine cones – the trail leads them to the Forest School area, surrounded by police tape. Back in the classroom the children decide they need to make 'wanted' posters and Jo helps them to put these up around the school. For several days, until Henry is 'rescued', the class are busy writing letters, police reports and 'journalism'. Even after Henry is returned the writing continues as Jo muses 'I wonder how Henry felt when he was kidnapped?' and children create diaries imagining his experiences.

Autonomy, or the ability to manage ones own actions and become self-directed rather than being governed by external control, is an important aspect of the executive functions that underpin cognitive processes (see Chapter 2). The social context of classrooms may promote autonomous motivation or be controlling depending on the teacher's orientation. Some adults believe it is their job to ensure children do things correctly, make clear that children should do as they are told and see to it that they do. The ability to adapt to school demands in this way is often seen as an important element of school readiness. Controlling contexts pressurise children to think, act or feel in particular ways through external measures and language like 'have to' and 'should'.

Autonomy-supportive teachers, on the other hand, nurture and involve children's psychological needs and values. They do this by listening carefully, arranging resources and seating to encourage activity rather than passivity, creating opportunities for children to talk and work in their own way, treating their perspectives with respect and involving them in decision-making. Jo's approach supports autonomy. Children's interests are not neglected or frustrated but they experience volition and choice: she motivates them rather than coercing them into writing. Teachers such as Jo, and earlier Nick, believe it is important for children to initiate behaviours and try to solve problems for themselves rather than relying on adults to tell them what to do. Children who demonstrate these traits are well-placed to engage in academic learning so are truly ready for school. Jo was astonished at how much writing her class produced in connection with Henry's alleged kidnapping but it is evident that children's inner motivation, deriving from their own interest and concerns, created a self-perpetuating enthusiasm to record and communicate in writing. In terms of literacy, information needs to be placed in contexts of current interest that are meaningful to young children. This means direct instruction of vocabulary or phonology may not be productive (Snow 2006). Snow argues that supporting children to write, with their own attempts at spelling, reinforces phonological awareness as effectively as explicit curricula. Such learning, brought about through children's autonomous motivation, is more effective and long-lasting than reluctant engagement in writing activities to meet curriculum demands, an issue when children are not developmentally ready.

Autonomy-supporting teachers recognise learners' perspectives and this is important for children's well-being. They acknowledge children's occasionally negative emotional responses, conveying the value of activities that may seem uninteresting and providing meaningful reasons if choice must be restricted. Children will sometimes not want to conform to expectations but denying the validity of such reactions, or attempting to counter them, suggests to children that their feelings are unacceptable and should be adjusted to conform to the teacher's viewpoint. Recognising children's negative responses supports them in managing emotions productively rather than undermining their sense of autonomy and emotional competence. The difference this makes is evident in children's motivation towards academic learning – palpable in their curiosity, attempts at self-initiated mastery, greater persistence and readiness to face challenges independently. When teachers interpret children's agency as something requiring containment, then adult control has the effect of increasing compliance but reducing genuine involvement (Payler 2007). Negative emotions brought about through a controlling environment make children anxious and distracted, likely to attract even greater levels of external control. Formal attempts to produce readiness in children are therefore likely to be counterproductive because the level of control entailed distorts young children's experiences and works against the very characteristics that sustain genuine learning.

Whilst environments that encourage autonomy are important to support children's emotional responses and level of confidence, their own ideas about intelligence also affect their perceptions of themselves as learners. Dweck (2006) has shown that children with a fixed theory of intelligence assume that if learning needs effort then they cannot be intelligent. This leads them to focus on performance, such as good grades, rather than on the processes of learning. On the other hand, children with a growth theory of intelligence see it as an incremental quality that can be improved by effort. These children take on learning goals rather than performance ones and are prepared to try harder if they struggle with something. This leads to a mastery orientation rather than learned helplessness. Dweck suggests that children's beliefs about intelligence can be altered by feedback from adults who should praise effort rather than performance as this increases children's motivation to learn. Timely and carefully judged feedback also encourages children to reflect on their performance, supporting growing awareness of their own learning strategies.

Implications of technology

Young children are immersed in media and digital technologies from a very early age and this makes popular culture an important context for learning. Because they are accustomed to multi-modal forms of expression, tools such as cameras, tablets and smartphones are just as important communicative tools for children as pencils and paper were to earlier generations – note how Jo took it for granted that *all* these resources should be available to support literacy practices in her class.

Information and communications technology (ICT) reinforces social interaction and active learning; indeed it is valuable to all the key ingredients of effective pedagogy discussed in this chapter and aids development of children's metacognition (Wolfe and Flewitt 2010). Technology does not bring about learning by itself, however, and adults need to plan carefully and scaffold children's learning so as not to waste the potential that it offers. ICT is strongly motivational, affording opportunities for co-construction and sustained shared thinking when teachers use it as a medium for collaborative learning (Roberts-Holmes 2014). Unfortunately some teachers still equate 'playing on the computer' with letter and number recognition exercises and the like that are merely an attempt to disguise uninteresting activities, have little meaning to children and are certainly not play. Under these circumstances it is not surprising that Marsh (2010) identifies a disparity between young children's cultural identities in the home, where they are confident and able users of technology, and early years settings where experiences can be far less satisfactory.

Conclusion

Most of the debates about children's learning can be traced to different perceptions of the *purpose* of early childhood provision, reflected in curriculum frameworks drawn up for providers. Many European countries see early childhood as an extension of home life, placing more emphasis on continuing unfolding of children's emotional, social and physical development through holistic pedagogies that reinforce children's engagement in learning. On the other hand, policy-makers in England and the USA view early childhood as a phase of preparation for school when young children should be made ready for stages to follow. This position emphasises the development of linguistic and cognitive skills through a prescriptive curriculum and formal teaching. Provision of a curriculum alone does not meet the needs of early years and primary school children who require a more holistic approach in these crucial years of development. The English curriculum, especially at Key Stage 1, is overloaded with content at the expense of child-initiated exploration and learning. Under these circumstances, where classrooms are dominated by specific learning outcomes, it is too easy for learning to become passive rather than actively engaging children. Information that is 'taught' is not necessarily understood or retained. Children will more easily internalise new knowledge when it is linked to their interests and what they already know. Rather than a curricular framework of content, to be transmitted in lessons, a pedagogy is needed that starts from children's own experiences, their curiosity and choices. The aims of such a pedagogy are process-related rather than focused on content and emphasise the acquisition of dispositions and learning skills needed for lifelong learning, not just to pass short-term standardised tests.

The main goal of early years education should be the development of executive functions that are strongly indicative of school success (McClelland and Wanless 2015). Over time, children become able to regulate their own social, emotional and cognitive functions rather then relying on adult support. Teachers can foster children's ability to self-regulate by providing playful learning activities which reinforce communication skills, negotiation, decision-making and taking others' perspectives into account (Kangas et al. 2015). Children with poor executive functions have problems paying attention and completing tasks; they struggle to inhibit impulsive behaviours and so may be disruptive in class. School may be less enjoyable for them because they find compliance with school demands difficult and their teachers may become frustrated with them. These children are likely to be viewed as not yet ready for school, although Kangas et al. (2015) argue that it is not helpful to regard readiness as something a child does or does not possess. All children have potential in the right circumstances where attention is paid to the contexts and environment for learning.

A child-centred social pedagogy provides the conditions in which young children thrive and learn. This includes playful contexts where children experience appropriate levels of cognitive challenge and sensitive support from adults with high expectations who are clear about their purpose and role (Moyles et al. 2002).

A sense of individual autonomy and personal motivation is generated when children feel a measure of control over events and activities. This encourages a sense that they are effective, capable learners, leading to self-directed learning rather than being compelled to take part. Too often classrooms are dominated by teachers' talk but children need ample opportunities to speak, reflect on their own learning and gain understanding of their own cognition. Conversational dialogue is important to foster children's capacity for abstract thought as well as their retention and understanding of knowledge.

When children are supported to acquire perseverance in working at tasks, skills to focus and maintain attention, and capacity to hold information in mind long enough to associate one concept with another, they are able to acquire academic content: in other words, they are ready for school. Furthermore, when they are motivated and believe themselves to be competent learners, they will persist, stay focused and exert effort to do this. By contrast, if they are led to memorise content without the skills to apply appropriate strategies by themselves, their progress is at risk. Similarly if they find the learning environment hostile or the content meaningless and too difficult, they are less likely to exert sufficient effort. Early education that transmits academic content to children but leaves them detesting or frustrated by school, or nervous or fearful in the school environment, has let young children down. It is the children who feel they have autonomy, competence and good relationships within the school environment who will become effective learners and well-adjusted citizens.

References

Bigelow, A.E., MacLean, K. and Proctor, J. (2004) The role of joint attention in the development of infants' play with objects, *Developmental Science*, Vol 7 (4): 419–421.

Bingham, S. and Whitebread, D. (2012) *School readiness: a critical review of perspectives and evidence*. Report prepared for TACTYC, available at www.tactyc.org/projects/. Accessed June 25, 2016.

Bruner, J. (1977) *The process of education*, Cambridge, MA: Harvard University Press.

Dahlberg, G. and Moss, P. (2005) *Ethics and politics in early childhood education*, London: Routledge Falmer.

Donaldson, M. (1978) *Children's minds*, London: Fontana Press.

Dweck, C.S. (2006) *Mindset: the new psychology of success*, New York: Random House.

Fisher, J. (2016) *Interacting or Interfering? Improving interactions in the early years*, Maidenhead: Open University Press.

Goswami, U. (2015) *Children's cognitive development and learning*, York: Cambridge Primary Review Trust.

Hirsh-Pasek, K., Golinkoff, R.M., Berk, L. and Singer, D. (2009) *A mandate for playful learning in preschool: presenting the evidence*, New York: Oxford University Press.

Howard, J. (2010) Making the most of play in the early years: understanding and building on children's perceptions, in P. Broadhead, J. Howard and E. Wood (eds), *Play and learning in the early years: research into practice*, London: Sage.

Kangas, J., Ojala, M. and Venninen, T. (2015) Children's self-regulation in the context of participatory pedagogy in early childhood education, *Early Education and Development*, Vol 26 (5–6): 847–870.

Marsh, J. (2010) *Childhood, creativity and culture: a literature review*, Sheffield University, available at www.creativitycultureeducation.org/research-impact/literature-reviews/. Accessed June 25, 2016.

McClelland, M. and Wanless, S. (2015) Introduction to the special issue: self-regulation across different cultural contexts, *Early Education and Development*, Vol 26 (5–6): 609–614.

Moyles, J. (ed) (2010) *Thinking about play: developing a reflective approach*, Maidenhead: Open University Press.

Moyles, J., Adams, S. and Musgrove, A. (2002) *SPEEL study of pedagogical effectiveness in early learning* (DfES research report 363), London: DfES.

Murray, J. (2015) Early childhood pedagogies: spaces for young children to flourish, *Early Childhood Development and Care*, Vol 185 (11–12): 1715–1732.

Neitzel, C. and Stright, A.D. (2003) Relations between mothers' scaffolding and children's academic self-regulation: establishing a culture of self-regulatory competence, *Journal of Family Psychology*, Vol 17: 147–159.

Organisation for Economic Co-operation and Development (OECD) (2006) *Starting strong II: early childhood education and care*, Paris: OECD.

Payler, J. (2007) Opening and closing interactive spaces: shaping four-year-old children's participation in two English settings, *Early Years*, Vol 27 (3): 237–254.

Piaget, J. (1972) Some aspects of operations, in M. Piers (ed), *Play and development*, New York: W.W. Norton.

Rinaldi, C. (2006) *In dialogue with Reggio Emilia: listening, researching and learning*, London: Routledge.

Roberts-Holmes, G. (2014) Playful and creative ICT pedagogical framing: a nursery school case study, *Early Child Development and Care*, Vol 184 (1): 1–14.

Siraj-Blatchford, I., Sylva, K., Muttock, S., Gilden, R. and Bell, D. (2002) *Researching effective pedagogy in the early years (REPEY)*, DfES Research Report 356, London: DfES/HMSO.

Snow, C.E. (2006) What counts as literacy in early childhood? In K. McCartney and D. Phillips (eds), *Blackwell handbook of early childhood development*, Oxford: Blackwell.

Stephen, C. (2010) Pedagogy: the silent partner in early years learning, *Early Years*, Vol 30 (1): 15–28.

Sylva, K., Melhuish, E., Sammons, P., Siraj-Blatchford, I. and Taggart, B. (2004) *The effective provision of pre-school education (EPPE) project: final report*, London: Institute of Education.

Trevarthen, C. and Aitken, K. (2001) Infant intersubjectivity: research, theory and clinical applications, *The Journal of Child Psychology and Psychiatry and Allied Disciplines*, Vol 42 (1): 3–48.

Vygotsky, L. (1978) *Mind in society*, Cambridge, MA: Harvard University Press.

Wall, S., Litjens, I. and Taguma, M. (2015) *Early childhood education and care pedagogy review: England*, OECD, available at www.oecd.org/unitedkingdom/early-childhood-education-and-care-pedagogy-review-england.pdf. Accessed June 25, 2016.

Weldermariam, K. T. (2014) Cautionary tales on interrupting children's play: a study from Sweden, *Childhood Education*, Vol 90 (4): 265–271.

Winsler, A. and Naglieri, J.A. (2003) Overt and covert verbal problem-solving strategies: developmental trends in use, awareness, and relations with task performance in children aged 5 to 17, *Child Development*, Vol 74: 659–678.

Wolfe, S. and Flewitt, R. (2010) New technologies, new multimodal literacy practices and young children's metacognitive development, *Cambridge Journal of Education*, Vol 40 (4): 387–399.

Worthington, M. and van Oers, B. (2016) Pretend play and the cultural foundations of mathematics, *European Early Childhood Education Research Journal*, Vol 24 (1): 51–66.

4

THE DIVERSITY OF CHILDREN'S EARLY EXPERIENCES

Introduction

The make-up of society in the UK is complex and there are significant differences in the environment and opportunities that young children will encounter. Since development is so integrated with social context (Bronfenbrenner 1979), every child will have a different combination of biological, cognitive and motivational elements affecting their readiness for formal school learning. This makes recognition of, and provision for, children's diversity crucial to their likelihood of future success. There is no standard childhood and the quality of relationships experienced by young children, as well as the amount of cognitive stimulation they receive and spoken language that they hear, will have a substantial effect on their development and ability to cope with learning outside the home. Other equally important factors are the physical environment, including good nutrition and health care, adequate housing and the type of neighbourhood in which they grow up. These differences affect early development and continue to impact children as they get older, influencing both self-concept and disposition towards learning. Consequently children begin school with a wide variation in skill levels that affects subsequent progress and learning and how ready they are perceived to be.

A range of different factors support healthy child development but equally it can be compromised by adverse circumstances. The UK is one of the most unequal societies in Europe, reported by the Organisation for Economic Co-operation and Development (OECD) as having a more pronounced impact on children's educational achievement than any of the 52 countries studied (Machin 2006). Regardless of background and opportunity, the fixed yardstick of 'readiness' that young children are measured against leads to many being labelled as deficient in some way and this can impede teachers' abilities to see children's potential. The Cambridge Primary Review (Alexander 2010) found that 'deficit thinking' from some teachers plays a part in underachievement of black, Bangladeshi and Pakistani children, white working-class boys and Travellers. It is important to remember that 'difference' does not imply 'deficit' and to focus on, and value, what each individual child brings with them. Vandenbroeck (2010) warns of the need to think beyond stereotypical assumptions that particular social categories or ethnic families do not value education enough. The reality is more complex and narrow education perspectives fail to take into account broader dimensions of access and curriculum that immigrant or minority ethnic children may need to succeed. This chapter considers children from Traveller communities and those whose mother tongue is not English, who may already be very adept at one or more languages whilst learning English. It explores the implications of background, culture and socio-economic circumstances with particular attention to the consequences of growing up in poverty. Differential experiences of supportive family and community networks, social capital and parenting skills that young children may encounter are taken into account and the importance of the home as a learning environment is examined in relation to the current emphasis on parenting.

Gypsy, Roma and Traveller children

Across Europe two groups of children are notable as particularly disadvantaged, growing up in conditions of extreme poverty – these are immigrant and Traveller and Gypsy Roma children. These groups also have the lowest access to provision (Bennett 2012) and so often lack visibility. Foster and Norton (2012) claim that, despite a robust legal framework for educational equality, the UK has a long way to go before this is achieved for Gypsy, Roma and Traveller (GRT) communities. Many teachers and early years practitioners have little experience with Traveller families and limited knowledge or understanding of their lives and culture and so may have difficulty meeting their needs. Adults' negative attitudes towards GRT communities, including towards children themselves (Bennett 2012; CPR 2010) are also damaging. These factors all contribute to the fact that GRT children make up the lowest achieving minority ethnic group at all key stages (Wilkin et al. 2010). There are many reasons for this, including lack of experience of the educational system amongst parents; social and economic issues; disrupted educational experience; widespread racist bullying; low teacher expectations and lack of cultural sensitivity within the education system. Often multiple factors interact and combine to undermine children's ability to fulfil their potential.

It is the opportunity, not the *ability* to learn that children from GTR communities lack. Inclusive practices that create a positive climate and recognise others' perspectives (Bennett 2012; CPR 2010) can go a long way to offset difficulties. Young children and their parents need to feel accepted and a sense of belonging so, as with every child, family background and culture must be taken into account in constructing the curriculum. Two examples observed within my local school area illustrate very different responses to young children from Traveller communities.

Ivan was enrolled in the Reception class of his local village school. Although largely lacking educational experience themselves, his parents were very supportive of him going to school. Over the first couple of days the class teacher became increasingly concerned about Ivan's lack of fine motor skills – he couldn't manipulate a pair of scissors, had never handled a pencil and seemed unfamiliar and uninterested in Lego. She contacted the Traveller Education Service as a matter of urgency and a family liaison worker agreed to visit the family to discuss the issue. Arriving at the site, the first thing the liaison worker noticed was Ivan helping his Dad strip down a car engine, expertly taking apart and replacing screws, nuts and spark plugs. In fact Ivan had very well-developed fine motor skills but applied them in a quite different context to that expected of a four-year-old boy by the teacher.

Mrs C. is used to Traveller children in her Year 1 class and makes sure the curriculum is meaningful for them through careful planning. She sought advice about extending the books available in the classroom from the Traveller Education Service and has provided a number of resources such as a wooden trailer that all the children in the class like to play with. In a recent project about Families, she made sure that all children's backgrounds and circumstances were acknowledged and valued. Aware that some parents are hostile towards the Traveller community, she hopes this inclusion will not only benefit GTR children but also that the rest of the class will develop tolerance through familiarity and understanding of different lifestyles.

Ivan's teacher was well-meaning; she was genuinely concerned to help him and worried that what she perceived to be his lack of fine motor skills would impede his ability to make progress in school. Unfortunately her deficit view combined with a narrow perspective of readiness meant that she underestimated his skills and focused only on what he lacked. Should Ivan continue to be regarded as a problem through school then his chances of engaging positively in educational opportunities will be curtailed. If he had been in Mrs C.'s class, however, he would have a much greater chance of success. Complete absence of any material related to Gypsies and Travellers within the National Curriculum has been cited as contributing to a feeling from GRT communities that formal education is of limited practical use. Bowers (cited in Foster and Norton 2012) points out that 'in schools, children learn more about the Romans, Vikings or even fairies than they do about our cultures and what we have contributed to this world' (p. 105). Mrs C. works hard to ensure that the curriculum the students in her class experience is inclusive of all. Rather than viewing Traveller children as problems to be managed or overcome, her school makes sure that provision matches children's needs. For instance, they recognise young children from transient communities sometimes feel confined indoors and prefer to read and write in the playground shelter where they feel more secure and comfortable. They keep a collection of spare school sweatshirts so that children passing through the area can still feel a sense of belonging. In particular they are aware that developing relationships of trust through dialogue with families and community groups is necessary to break down barriers and ensure all parties are 'ready' for children to attend school.

Ethnicity and second language learners

Britain has always been an ethnically diverse country but in recent years increasing numbers of bilingual children, many of whom do not speak English, are entering early years settings. Twelve per cent of school children in the UK are identified as having a mother tongue other than English and this number rises to 50 per cent in urban areas such as inner London. In some London primary schools 80 per cent of children are classified as bilingual and more than 200 languages are spoken in their homes (Drury 2013). Given that there is such an intimate connection between language, social interaction and cognitive processing this has significant implications for young bilingual or multilingual learners, for practitioners and for settings.

Bilingual children are those operating in more than one language. It refers to the situation rather than their speaking ability as there may be considerable differences between children in both fluency and ability to understand what is said to them. As the section on language development in Chapter 2 demonstrates, children start to learn *about* language long before they begin to talk. Many children interact in two (or more) languages in everyday life even though they may not necessarily express themselves in one – or indeed any – language yet, because comprehension is always considerably in advance of spoken ability. There are many differences amongst bilingual/multilingual children and it is important to recognise each child's individuality and not view them as a homogeneous group.

> Ali, Bilal, Hassan and Andrej attend the nursery attached to a Children's Centre in a large Midlands town. The boys' ages range from 3.5 years (Bilal) to 4.2 years (Hassan). Andrej is Romanian; he and his mother arrived in England a few months ago. The two of them live alone in a small flat and the mother recently began work as a translator. The other three all belong to the local Punjabi community, speaking Pushto at home with their families. Although they understand some English and respond when the teacher speaks to them, only Hassan has ever been heard to say anything in English himself. The three boys play together regularly; they are particularly keen on construction and spend whole mornings building complex structures. Hassan appears to take the lead, instructing the other two who look to him for guidance. They chatter together as they work and, although the teacher cannot follow what they are saying, it is clear they are making up their own narratives that they act out through their play.
>
> Andrej, on the other hand, tends to wander round the nursery with little recognisable purpose. He stands and watches other children but does not join in with them and they never initiate any kind of social interaction with him.

When he first started at nursery he tried to talk to adults and the other children in his home language but, after a week or so when this did not work, he fell silent. Although he does not appear actively distressed, nor does he show any particular interest in what is going on and the teacher is concerned at his lack of engagement. Andrej's mother has said her son likes to draw so the teacher has provided pastels and charcoal in addition to the usual drawing materials. Although he does not show any change of attitude, Andrej has started to take paper and a box of pastels to a table on his own where he sits quietly mumbling to himself.

The Children's Centre has managed to access funding to pay for a bilingual teaching assistant (TA) who works part time at the nearby Primary school to do two sessions a week at the nursery. The teacher expects this to help the three Pushto-speaking boys to become more integrated but she is struggling to support Andrej. She has heard that young bilinguals usually undergo a 'silent period' and is hoping that, as Andrej starts to pick up English, he will begin to make friends.

Young children are capable of learning several languages at once and indeed, considered globally, it is the monolingual child who is in the minority; 60 per cent of the world's children speak at least two languages. As language is initially acquired through social interaction in the home, this is a straightforward and natural process for children from bilingual families who grow up hearing and using both languages in daily use. Yet the fact that language acquisition is a natural process can sometimes hide its complexity, and building communication with children who come from homes where English is not spoken requires deliberate action rather than just being left to chance. Children first need to learn the rhythm of the language and become used to the sounds they hear around them. Like Ali, Bilal and Hassan, they may understand what is said to them but it can take time to build confidence to speak out loud. In addition children may have to learn new cultural norms and interpret what is going on. This is true of all children entering a new setting where the 'rules' of the context are unknown to them, but it is inevitably more difficult if a child encounters the situation through the medium of another language (Brooker 2002). These factors clearly influence their readiness for schooling environments.

The complexity of young bilinguals' learning is often overlooked because it is assumed that they will quickly pick up English naturally, but this assumption disregards the crucial importance of social context for language development. Accordingly, young children are often involved in a 'double bind' (Tabors 1997) whereby they are not able to engage in social interaction because of their lack of English, yet the absence of social interaction means they miss opportunities to hear and practice language. Consequently young children are likely to spend time playing alone silently or humming, singing and talking to themselves – this is the 'silent period' that Andrej's teacher recognises. Though an acknowledged stage in development of a second or additional language, Drury (2013) argues that 'non-verbal' is a more appropriate term for this period when the child is acclimatising to the new environment. She points out that the 'silent' period can carry negative overtones implying some form of deficit in a child (for instance, it is noticeable that the teacher mentions Andrej's 'attitude' and is concerned at his failure to engage rather than her failure to engage him). During the non-verbal period young children collect information about the new language; they may begin to rehearse to themselves, and, in time, to practise in private speech before becoming confident enough to utter individual words and phrases. Drury (2013) emphasises the need for reassurance and encouragement during this period as it is important that a child knows they are an accepted member of the group. As affective and cognitive aspects of development are so closely linked (see Chapter 2), Andrej's potential for learning may be inhibited by the emotional tensions of adapting to a different cultural environment. Unlike the other three boys who are part of the local community, migrant children such as Andrej have additional issues to contend with. Many will be living in insecure circumstances, remote from extended family and familiar environments. Some may have suffered trauma and extremely disturbing experiences that inevitably affect holistic development. Attending nursery, playgroup or school represents their first step into society and so has a marked impact on their self-concept. As Vandenbroeck notes:

> [ECEC] presents them with a mirror on how society looks at them and thus how they may look at themselves, since it is only in the context of sameness and difference that identity can be constructed. It is in this public mirror that they are confronted with these essential and existential questions: Who am I? And is it OK to be who I am? (2010: 83)

Adult engagement is crucial in developing opportunities for young bilinguals to interact socially with their peers. Resources alone are not sufficient and although Andrej's teacher provides materials to support his interest in drawing she fails to follow this through, perhaps by sitting and sketching with him, or even better, by involving him in a drawing activity with a small group of other children. Adults should never pressurise children to speak but can model language by continuing to talk even when children don't respond, interpreting and acknowledging non-verbal responses. They need to provide a running commentary on what is happening and what the child is doing in the same way as for pre-verbal infants; this offers the child a model, providing words, phrases and language patterns before children are able to utter for themselves. Unfortunately the majority of early years practitioners in the UK are monolingual themselves, and can lack confidence in supporting second language learning. Consequently many young bilinguals' interaction with staff is largely confined to classroom management, limiting opportunities for cognitive development. This is evident with the three Punjabi boys in the case study above – although benefiting from interaction with each other, by leaving them to play alone the teacher curbs their learning. They are missing out on possibilities for sustained shared thinking with an adult who could extend and develop their knowledge and concepts. Such opportunities are regularly available to their English-speaking classmates and failing to provide the same chances for Hassan and his friends is likely to impact on both current development and later attainment.

For these reasons early years settings often rush to encourage children to use English only, but such a strategy, though well-meaning in intent, is ill-advised. Children's control of their own mental processing and performance incorporates emotional experiences and social abilities as much as cognitive processes, and this underlies learning, thinking, reasoning and remembering. The support of their home language is very important in facilitating young children's overall language and cognitive development; children need to establish and fully embed their learning cognitively before attempting to express their ideas in another language. The EYFS specifically notes that 'providers must take reasonable steps to provide opportunities for children to develop and use their home language in play and learning, supporting their language development at home' (DfE 2014: paragraph 1.7). Involvement of a bilingual TA will act as a bridge between the language and culture of home and setting for Ali, Bilal and Hassan, enabling them to build on their strengths, interests and capabilities in language that is already familiar to them whilst also providing structured support for English language learning; Andrej is not so lucky. Having access to a second language, and therefore more than one symbolic, conceptual system supports cognitive flexibility and under optimal conditions is greatly advantageous for a child. But the early stages of language learning are complex, requiring a supportive environment and appropriate social interaction to foster children's overall development and therefore their readiness for school.

Challenges associated with learning, teaching and assessment in a language in which they may be less competent explains why children from other language backgrounds sometimes struggle at school. Language is not the only factor affecting educational attainment of children from minority ethnic families however; socio-economic status (SES) has the greatest influence on children's outcomes, particularly affecting those from Pakistani and Bangladeshi backgrounds (Coghlan et al. 2009). Whilst it must be borne in mind that population averages obscure wide variations in class and background, nonetheless, poverty is higher amongst all black and minority ethnic groups who are paid less on average than the majority white population with similar qualifications and experience (Barnard and Turner 2011). A complex interplay of factors together creates an adverse effect on development and learning of young children but the most pervasive is growing up in challenging social and economic circumstances. SES has a cumulative effect on children's development and whilst children of wealthier parents with low developmental scores have a tendency to catch up, and may even overtake, children from low-income backgrounds with higher scores, large numbers of children born to low-earning parents are likely to remain disadvantaged throughout their lives (Feinstein 2003).

The effects of poverty and social deprivation

Across Europe, young children are at greater risk of poverty and social exclusion than the adult population in all countries other than Denmark, Finland, Norway, Slovenia and Sweden (Bennett 2012). Within the UK vast inequality in material wealth means unequal access to resources in terms of living conditions, educational opportunities and healthcare. In addition, limited income can affect opportunities for supportive family and community networks, social capital and the ability to parent. Abundant evidence suggests that inequality stemming from SES is associated with a multitude of developmental outcomes for children, ranging from low birth weight and increased likelihood of mothers' postnatal depression to irregular bed-times and the probability of being read to daily (Marmot 2010).

> Lisa lives with her partner Dave and young son Daniel in a two bedroomed flat in the inner city. Daniel is just three and Lisa is 7 months pregnant with a second child. Dave lost his previous job as a driver when the company he worked for went out of business; he now works for a large store meaning frequent evening and weekend work. Neither he nor Lisa are happy with the irregular hours that leave them little time together as a family, but on the other hand it gives Dave flexibility to be able to take Daniel to nursery some mornings and let Lisa have a rest. Lisa is finding this pregnancy harder than her first; she feels tired all the time and worries about the future. She has been working as a care assistant in a nursing home because the hours fit in with looking after Daniel but will be finishing work in a few weeks. She worries about how they will manage without her wage as they already struggle to pay the bills.
>
> Lisa has missed her last two appointments at the maternity clinic, a twenty-minute bus ride away. By the time she has finished work and collected Daniel from nursery it seems too much of an effort to get there and back again. Anyway, she tells herself, this is her second child and she knows what to expect; better to spend the time with Daniel who has been playing up a lot recently.

Approximately 3.5 million children are currently classified as living in poverty in the UK, amounting to 27 per cent of all children (NCB 2013) and, contrary to popular prejudice, the majority of these children live in families where at least one family member is working. It is estimated that by 2020 one in four UK children will be in poverty (Institute for Fiscal Studies 2013), a condition that negatively affects every aspect of their lives in material, educational, social and psychological terms (Hansen et al. 2010; Ridge 2011). Poverty also creates parental stress with repercussions for parent–child interactions and so impacts on children's language acquisition and their ability to self-regulate. The implications of economic disadvantage for children's cognitive and socio-emotional outcomes have been recognised in development of the UK's first national child poverty strategy for 2011–2014 (DWP and DfE 2011), recently updated for 2014–2017 (HMG 2014). Official policy is underpinned by a number of government reports and reviews including the Field Report (2010) on poverty, the Allen Review (2011) regarding early intervention and the Marmot Review (2010) of health inequalities in the UK.

Healthy development is likely to be compromised for children living in deprived neighbourhoods with limited resources such as nursery schools, health facilities, parks and playgrounds. Not only are children from socially disadvantaged families less likely to be enrolled in preschool settings, but early years provision in poorer neighbourhoods is of lower quality with less qualified staff than in wealthier areas (Mathers et al. 2011). Only 16 per cent of PVI (private, voluntary and independent) settings in the most disadvantaged neighbourhoods are considered outstanding compared to 27 per cent in more affluent areas (Gambaro et al. 2013). It is now recognised that high-quality early childhood education improves children's well-being and can help reduce some of the effects of poverty, but evidently the very children who would most benefit are frequently missing out.

ECEC is a large part of government strategy in respect of poverty, as a means of narrowing the gap between poorer and wealthier children in the early years (DWP and DfE 2011: 43; HMG 2014: 14). Two main aspects of this approach encompass access and quality: firstly extension of free education places, already available for three- and four-year-old children, to provide 15 hours education and care to the most disadvantaged two-year-olds and secondly, continuing emphasis on graduate staff, recognised as a key indicator of quality in early childhood settings (Urban et al. 2011).

The relationship between poverty and physical development

Four months later, Lisa has had a baby girl, Amy. Dave is doing what he can to help but his working hours make it difficult. Last weekend they had planned a family day out but he was called in at the last minute to cover for an absent colleague; he cannot refuse because he knows jobs are hard to come by at the moment and besides, they need the money. He is aware that Lisa seems low in spirits but assumes this is just the effect of a new baby and she will soon be back to her usual self.

Lisa feels tired all the time. She tries to make sure that she sees to the baby during the night because Dave has work to go to, but she is struggling with lack of sleep. Lisa doesn't remember Daniel crying as much as Amy does and finds it hard to settle her. She is becoming short-tempered with Daniel and seems to shout at him for nothing in particular. She feels guilty and, as the weather is improving, decides to take the children to the park to try to make it up to him. It is a long walk and when they get there Lisa feels intimidated by a group of youths hanging around the swings. There is also a lot of broken glass and she is worried about Daniel hurting himself. Daniel whines all the way back and Amy starts to cry again so that Lisa is exhausted by the time they reach home.

Anxiety about money adds to Lisa's stress. Although she had only been earning the minimum wage, less money coming in makes it harder than ever to manage on their income. She shops carefully, buying low-budget, economy items in the supermarket but still struggles to make the money stretch and can rarely afford extras like fresh fruit.

A child's physical development is shaped by environmental influences before they are even born and life chances are likely to be greatly enhanced by the mother's physical and mental health as well as her access to a nutritious diet. Healthy birth weight has implications for physical well-being throughout life (Marmot 2010) but children born to low-income parents are more likely to be premature and have low birth weight. Moreover infant mortality is higher amongst children born into poverty. Access to health care services, including antenatal services, maternity care and developmental screenings, is more difficult for families with low incomes (Bamfield 2007). Lower rates of breastfeeding and higher rates of post-natal depression are also reported, with both of these having implications for babies' well-being: breastfeeding is thought to be connected with improved immunity, digestive health and better neurological development whilst post-natal depression may affect a mother's relationship with her child(ren).

As children grow older their own mental health may suffer and a number of studies connect growing up in a low-income household to poor mental health (Bingham and Whitebread 2012: section 2.2). Contributing factors include homelessness, frequent moves and inadequate or overcrowded housing conditions. Poor housing is likewise connected to a number of childhood health problems such as reduced resistance to respiratory infections and asthma. Children living in disadvantaged communities are also more likely to be exposed to environmental dangers such as crime, violence and drug misuse and have a higher rate of accidents and accidental death. In addition the relationship between poverty and childhood obesity has been well established and children from low-income households are more likely to have an inadequate diet and suffer from associated conditions such as anaemia and diabetes. Poor dental health is more prevalent and children at schools in socially disadvantaged areas have about 50 per cent more tooth decay than those in non-deprived schools (Hirsch 2007).

The relationship between poverty and cognitive and behavioural development

Growing up in poverty has serious implications for children's academic learning and school readiness; differences in educational outcomes by income and background are apparent from a young age so that by age 22 months children's development scores are seen as a predictor of later educational achievement (Feinstein 2003; Field 2010). Continual poverty in their early years has a cumulative impact on children's cognitive development and significantly lower test scores are seen at ages three, five and seven (Dickerson and Popli 2012). A recent report from Save the Children (2013) showed that young children from low-income families are more at risk of falling behind at school in key skills such as reading and are less likely to catch up in later years, so that most of the difference in GCSE results between rich and poor children has already been fixed by the age of seven. Bradbury (2014), however, warns of the role of assessment in constructing learner identities and argues that there is great potential for low expectations of some pupils to result in low attainment and set the child on a trajectory of educational failure.

A key explanatory factor in linking economic disadvantage to a range of poor cognitive outcomes is inadequate language acquisition. Averages are statistical measures applying across large social groups and many children from disadvantaged families show good language skills, but nonetheless below-average levels of language development are more commonly found in children growing up in low-income households. Data from the longitudinal Millennium Cohort Study of 18,000 children born around the turn of the century (Hansen et al. 2010), found that children from the most socio-economically disadvantaged groups are twice as likely to experience language delay (Law et al. 2015). Measurement of vocabulary shows wide disparity between children with those from most advantaged SES groups being more than a year ahead by age five (Blanden and Machin 2010). Although performance drops off gradually across social groups, there is marked difference between children in the top and bottom percentiles.

As speech, language and communication (SLC) progress in the early years is linked to outcomes in children's cognitive ability, literacy, social and emotional development, and child behaviour (Dockrell et al. 2007), it has implications for their capacity to engage in learning opportunities when they start school. Early Years Foundation Stage Profiles show that developmental measures in all areas of the curriculum are lower for disadvantaged children and only 36 per cent begin school with a good level of development, compared to 55 per cent of children from more economically favourable backgrounds (DfE 2013). The largest disparity is in terms of literacy skills with a 20 percentage point gap, so these children may lack the spoken language ability necessary to support reading and writing skills. A less visible concern, though of equal importance for children's academic success, is the effect of poor SLC on social and emotional development and behaviour as language plays a crucial role in the growth in self-regulation (Morrison 2015). Limited communication skills inhibit development of self-regulation so children who lack this ability may experience difficulties adapting and be deemed not 'ready' when they reach formal school age.

It is unsurprising that the ability to self-regulate is associated with socioeconomic status as not only do children growing up in poverty frequently lack the sort of environment that can encourage development of such skills, but they are also more likely to be subject to stress hormones that may inhibit cognitive functions and emotional control. Particular risk factors include low income, low occupational status, maternal depression, being an English language learner and/ or having a mother with a low education level (McClelland and Wanless 2015). Self-regulatory skills can be developed and improved during early childhood and several studies demonstrate significant gains and improved outcomes for intervention groups in comparison to control groups. Findings have been particularly strong for children from disadvantaged social groups (Blair and Raver 2015; Schmitt et al. 2015). It is important, however, to resist a deficit attitude to social and emotional development. Bennett (2012) recognises socio-emotional skills as an ongoing developmental task for each child as an individual. This touches on issues of personal identity, self-concept, inclusion and attitudes to society but is too often viewed superficially in terms of behaviours to facilitate class management and learning processes. Socio-emotional development should not be conceptualised simply as a matter of vulnerable children acquiring 'compliant social skills' or the 'socialisation of minority children into majority practices and values' (Bennett 2012: 52).

The effects of quality early years provision

Lisa is finding Amy much more demanding than she remembers Daniel being; she seems to cry a lot and doesn't settle when Lisa holds her. She has stopped taking Daniel to nursery. It was difficult getting him there on time in the mornings when she had to deal with the baby too and sometimes she would be late picking him up. The manager complained that late pick-ups disrupted staff and children's routines but Lisa wasn't prepared to explain as she found her manner intimidating. Anyway, she thinks, if she is at home all day with the baby then there's no need for childcare anymore. She tries to take the children out when she can because Daniel gets restless and difficult stuck inside the flat all day, but it isn't easy on the stairs with the buggy so she is glad when Dave is at home during the day to give her a hand.

One day the Health Visitor comes to check on the baby. It has been a particularly difficult day – Amy was awake for much of the night and Lisa is exhausted, Daniel spilled milk all over the table and now it looks like there is a problem with the washing machine. Lisa knows they can't afford to replace it as they're already a month behind on the rent and the gas bill is due. Sandra, the HV, assures Lisa that Amy is doing fine but says that it is her she is worried about. She asks some questions about how Lisa is coping, but Lisa assures her everything is fine. She is worried that if she admits to struggling she will be marked out as a bad mother. Sandra asks whether Lisa ever takes Daniel to the Children's Centre on the estate and mentions a mother and baby group that is starting up there. She leaves a leaflet with opening times and a list of what happens at the Children's Centre but Lisa ignores it. The last thing she needs now whilst her situation is so difficult is other people interfering; she feels sure that once Amy starts sleeping better then things will improve.

Quality early years provision has been linked to cognitive outcomes and appears to have a significant role in improving children's life chances: this is particularly effective for children from disadvantaged backgrounds (Melhuish et al. 2004). Within a market system, however, where parents' choices are affected by their purchasing power, opportunities to access high-quality provision may be restricted and quality is often weakest in areas of highest deprivation (Ofsted 2014) as the logic of for-profit services is to cater for more affluent districts and families (Vandenbroeck 2010). Despite provision of free places, take up amongst families living in poverty lags behind that of more affluent parents (NAO 2012). In recent years policy focus has moved from universal provision to more targeted services aimed at narrowing the gap for children from low-income families – as well as the two-year-old offer already noted, another initiative is the extension of Pupil Premium funding for additional resources to support vulnerable children. Though considerably less than the amount available for older children, the Early Years Pupil Premium (EYPP) offers some potential to enhance provision, for example through continuing professional development or outreach for parents. Mathers and Smees (2014) suggest that the most effective use of EYPP could be to support employment of graduate level staff as this is key to providing high-quality early years education. Only graduate leadership has been associated with a narrower gap between PVI settings located in deprived and more advantaged areas.

Engagement with parents

Although there are strong associations between a child's social background and educational success, poor results are not inevitable and a number of schools and nurseries in areas of high deprivation succeed in achieving good outcomes for vulnerable children (Ofsted 2014; Social Mobility and Child Poverty Commission 2014). The fact that these settings are identified as 'bucking the trend' indicates that the norm is often lower in areas of disadvantage. Schools may find it hard to recruit good teachers to challenging schools so that a downward spiral occurs with low ability groups receiving poorer teaching – resulting in low attainment, lower expectations and aspirations and poorer motivation amongst children and parents (DCSF 2009). A key factor among schools and settings that succeed in supporting achievement relative to other SES groups is a culture of high expectations for all children, challenging the tendency to stereotype pupils from low-income or ethnic families (Campbell 2013). Another major element is effective engagement with parents as parental interest in children's education is claimed to increase chances of moving out of poverty as an adult by 25 percentage points (Blanden 2006). Effective partnerships can help overcome barriers and support social mobility because parenting is a key mechanism by which poverty affects children's development and progress. Partnership may also help overcome unfavourable perceptions of children's readiness.

Working with parents can interrupt cycles of continuing low achievement by improving parenting capacity and better settings make a particular effort to engage with parents who themselves had bad experiences of education (Ofsted 2014). Ofsted inspectors report that Children's Centres are best at improving parents' confidence and their ability to provide a high-quality home learning environment (HLE). Services must be attuned to parental needs so a market system of early years provision is not good at involving low-income parents (Vandenbroeck and Lazzari 2014). Economically poor parents are often unfairly assumed to be poor at parenting and Simpson et al. (2015) show that many practitioners fail to recognise how structural inequalities affect disadvantaged children. A large proportion of those working with low-income families accepted neoliberal rhetoric positioning the poor as 'feckless' and largely responsible for their own poverty. In contrast, practitioners who did not assume a deficit model of parenting and understood poverty as something largely beyond the control of parents themselves had more success in engaging with parents. Parents can feel undermined and patronised by clumsy intervention practices. Building strong, reciprocal relationships requires respect and sensitivity on the part of practitioners and an inclusive ethos; conflicting values and beliefs are frequently reasons that parents do not access early years provision.

> Lisa had never intended going to the Children's Centre but came across the leaflet Sandra had left on a day she was particularly depressed, feeling trapped indoors with a crying baby and fretful child. Realising the mother and baby session was that afternoon she decided on impulse to get out of the flat. Rachel, the activities worker, made her feel welcome and was interested in Amy without making Lisa feel she was checking up on her. Lisa found herself telling Rachel how hard she found this baby compared to her first. Rachel was very understanding and introduced her to another mum, Janie, a single parent with children of a similar age to Amy and Daniel. Janie fetched Lisa a cup of tea and they sat and chatted, comparing experiences whilst the two older children played in the crèche. When Dave got home that evening he noticed that Lisa seemed a bit less tense and didn't get cross when Daniel couldn't find his pyjamas at bedtime.

> Lisa continued to go to the mother and baby group every week. She began to feel a little more positive about life and consequently found the children easier to deal with. Sometimes Sandra the HV dropped in to sessions so Lisa was able to check with her about giving Amy finger foods. She became good friends with Janie who invited her to bring Daniel round to play with her own son Leo. Janie, on benefits, found it hard to make ends meet and Lisa confided her own money worries. Janie told her a debt advisor visited the Children's Centre regularly. She reassured Lisa that he was really helpful and wouldn't judge her. Janie was thinking of signing up for a computer training class the centre planned to put on, hoping it would help her find a better job when the children were older; she asked Lisa to come with her for moral support. Meanwhile Daniel was enjoying the crèche and the crèche worker suggested Lisa register him with the Children's Centre nursery. She explained

to Lisa how it would help him to socialise with other children and support his language development for when he goes to school.

Research demonstrates that strong multi-agency partnerships are a crucial contributory factor in improving engagement with disadvantaged families (Grayson 2013). The resources offered can compensate to some extent for low-income families' frequently more limited networks and help develop social capital. Good partnerships provide support for parents in their daily lives, improving living conditions and, in the longer term, increasing their opportunity to escape poverty. Parents may be reluctant to access external support however, being wary of exposing their family life to the scrutiny, and possible condemnation, of strangers (Cowley 2012). Without poverty sensitivity, practitioners are unlikely to make inroads into supporting children from disadvantaged backgrounds (Simpson et al. 2015). Other features that make a difference are working with adults and children together across health, social care and education disciplines and rooting services in communities so they can respond to local needs (Eisenstadt 2012). Investment in social spending is an important element in tackling poverty and disadvantage (OECD 2011), but in recent years large-scale cuts in services and provision are curbing the ability of agencies to respond.

The importance of the home learning environment

The home learning environment (HLE) refers to the extent that parents engage in learning opportunities with their children. The EPPE project found that HLE has a greater influence on children's intellectual and social development than parental occupation, education or income. What parents *do* is more important than who they *are*, and a home environment that is supportive of learning can help counteract the effects of disadvantage in the early years (Sylva et al. 2004).

Parents' ability to create an environment that supports their child's development varies depending on parenting style, their own life experiences and level of education – mothers' educational levels are an especially strong influence (Coghlan et al. 2009). Activities such as reading stories, singing nursery rhymes and songs, drawing and painting or trips out to the library and places of interest all encourage children's learning and development. A child whose mother plays informally with him with letters and numbers, perhaps through sound games or cooking activities, is supporting his all-round development, curiosity and desire to learn. These informal experiences in the home are just as valuable, if not more so, than learning in the setting environment. Rather than explicit, planned instruction as in organised settings, parents mediate their child's involvement in the everyday practices of their cultural communities. Children learn from the routines of ordinary life through joint attention, modelling and scaffolding in activities such as sorting socks from the washing machine or shopping for groceries. Rogoff (2003) uses the term 'guided participation' to refer to this alternative form of collaborative learning occurring naturally within communities. In this way she differentiates it from the Vygotskian concept of the zone of proximal development, which refers to skills, practices and discourses evident within academic settings.

Guided participation highlights the influence of maternal education for a stimulating HLE as mothers with higher levels of qualification are more likely to use the kinds of language, skills and concepts that are valued in schools. Bingham and Whitebread (2012: section 2.2) point to the massive advantages or disadvantages of children's language experience as exemplified by the number of words they will have heard long before they begin preschool. An additional factor is the number of stories children have read to them in the home (Marmot 2010). Oral language skills are not only important for later literacy development and school success but also correlate negatively with behaviour problems (Blanden and Machin 2010). Sammons et al. (2002) identify a high-quality HLE as the most important influence on children's social behaviours leading to increased independence, cooperation and sociability with less anti-social behaviour.

Evidence such as this is behind initiatives for early intervention (Allen 2011) intended to support low-income families and enhance parenting capacity. Evaluation of the Early Head Start programme, combining home visits and centre-based interventions for families of children from birth up to three years old, found intervention increased both quantity and quality of parental interactions as well as children's social and cognitive development (Love et al. 2005). Barnes and Freude-Lagevardi (2003) advise that the most effective interventions include both parent and child together with a focus on improving interactions. This suggests that parenting behaviours can be learned and that enhanced skills bring about improved developmental outcomes, echoed in the findings of Nutbrown et al. (2005) in relation to literacy during the preschool period. Initiatives such as family literacy projects provide learning activities for children alongside parents and this participation has been seen to increase children's progress (Sabates 2008). Moreover, Asmussen and Weizel (2010) showed fathers' involvement in their children's learning to be statistically related to their children achieving higher results and influencing their disposition towards learning and school, with associated improved behaviour.

Yet we should also be wary of calls for intervention; well-intentioned measures to support young children can too easily be overtaken by political agendas seeking simplistic answers to complex social issues. Misinterpretation, or misrepresentation, of research evidence frequently serves to justify an ideological position of state intervention in families' lives, and in recent years this has particularly been the case with evidence from neuroscience. MacNaughton (2006) draws attention to the equity and diversity issues raised by brain research in assuming that equity of inputs to children can achieve equity of outcomes. She suggests this mistakenly places blame for unequal outcomes on inadequate early stimulation (p. 64). Such interpretations enable policy-makers to deflect attention from deep structural inequalities within society. 'Neuromania' (Tallis 2011) is increasingly evident in policy and public discourse, used to legitimate moral arguments, a situation Furedi refers to as 'prejudice masquerading as research' (2001: 155).

In a critique of the misuse of developmental neuroscience within the Allen Review (2011) and other recent policy documents, Wastell and White (2012) suggest that 'neuroscience is an intoxicating ingredient in contemporary UK policy' (p. 406) and moral panic about 'damaged brains' has profound implications for policy and practice.

Conclusion

This chapter has considered some of the evidence regarding the effects of young children's backgrounds on cognitive, physical and socio-emotional development and shown how this can impact on young children's actual and perceived readiness for school. Outcomes for children may be compromised by factors such as the nature of early relationships with parents and carers, the extent of cognitive stimulation and access to adequate nutrition, health care and environmental resources. Preschool children are particularly vulnerable to poverty, which is the greatest cause of poor developmental outcomes and subsequent low academic progress – mainly because living in poverty is liable to disrupt parent–child relationships with adverse consequences for children's language and socio-emotional development. The crucial role of language in young children's development makes it particularly important to provide support for children and families whose first language is not English. Some ethnic groups are more likely than their white counterparts to experience poverty and this combination of poverty and English as a second language is the most likely root of associations between ethnicity and child outcomes (Coghlan et al. 2009). Formosinho and Figueiredo (2014) highlight the importance of participative pedagogy to counteract curriculum uniformity that may not fit the needs of diverse populations. They stress the importance of building team capacity to work with all types of diversity.

Research indicates the most powerful way to counter the effects of persistent poverty is through positive parenting within the home as quality of the HLE has a greater influence on children's early learning than any other factor. Consequently current policy priority is a focus on family and community engagement (Taguma et al. 2012) with emphasis on working closely with parents to enhance parenting capability. A positive HLE may partially compensate but cannot eliminate disadvantage. Whilst work with families is an important initiative – and clearly a more positive perspective than one that considers effects of background to be fixed – this approach requires sensitivity and understanding. Locating child poverty in the 'problem' behaviour of parents (Levitas 2012) disregards entrenched, structural reasons for poverty such as poorly paid and insecure work. Poverty often runs in families, transmitted from one generation to the next, and to break this chain of disadvantage requires a flexible and inclusive approach. Broad-based, integrated services working within a spirit of genuine partnership that fully recognises, values and responds to the cultural and socio-economic conditions of children's everyday lives have been shown to be most effective (Vandenbroeck and Lazzari 2014).

References

Alexander, R. (2010) *Children, their world, their education: final report and recommendations of the Cambridge Primary Review*, London: Routledge.

Allen, G. (2011) *Early intervention: the next steps*. London: Cabinet Office.

Asmussen, K. and Weizel, K. (2010) *Evaluating the evidence: fathers, families and children*, London: National Academy of Parenting Research.

Bamfield, L. (2007) *Born unequal: why we need a progressive pre-birth agenda*, London: Fabian Society.

Barnard, H. and Turner, C. (2011) *Poverty and ethnicity: a review of evidence*, York: Joseph Rowntree Foundation.

Barnes, J. and Freude-Lagevardi, A. (2003) *From pregnancy to early childhood: early interventions to enhance the mental health of children and families*, London: Mental Health Foundation.

Bennett, J. (2012) *Roma Early Childhood Inclusion: the RECI overview report, a joint initiative of the Open Society Foundations, the Roma Education Fund and UNICEF*, Budapest: OSF/REF/UNICEF.

Bingham, S. and Whitebread, D. (2012) *School readiness: a critical review of perspectives and evidence*. Report prepared for TACTYC, available at www.tactyc.org/projects/. Accessed June 25, 2016.

Blair, C. and Raver, C.C. (2015) School readiness and self-regulation: a developmental psychobiological approach, *Annual Review of Psychology*, Vol 66: 711–731.

Blanden, J. (2006) *'Bucking the trend': what enables those who are disadvantaged in childhood to succeed later in life?*, London: DWP Working Paper No. 31.

Blanden, J. and Machin, S. (2010) Changes in inequality and intergenerational mobility in early years assessments, in K. Hansen, H. Joshi and S. Dex (eds), *Children of the 21st century: the first five years*, Bristol: Policy Press.

Bradbury, A. (2014) Early childhood assessment: observation, teacher 'knowledge' and the production of attainment data in early years settings, *Comparative Education*, Vol 50 (3): 322–339.

Bronfenbrenner, U. (1979) *The ecology of human development*, Cambridge, MA: Harvard University Press.

Brooker, L. (2002) *Starting school: young children learning cultures*, Buckingham: Open University Press.

Cambridge Primary Review (CPR) (2010) *Cambridge Primary Review briefings: the final report*, available at www.primaryreview.org.uk. Accessed June 25, 2016.

Campbell, T. (2013) *Stereotyped at seven? Biases in teacher judgements of pupils' ability and attainment* (CLS Working Paper 2013/8), London: The Centre for Longitudinal Studies.

Coghlan, M., Bergeron, C., While, K., Sharp, C., Morris, M. and Rutt, S. (2009) *Narrowing the gap in outcome for poorer children through effective practice in the early years*, London: The Centre for Excellence and Outcomes in Children and Young People's Services (C4EO).

Cowley, M. (2012) Parenting policy and skills strategies, in L. Miller and D. Hevey (eds), *Policy issues in the early years*, London: Sage.

Department for Children, Schools and Families (DCSF) (2009), *Deprivation and education: the evidence on pupils in England, Foundation Stage to Key Stage 4*, London: HMSO.

Department for Education (DfE) (2013) *More great childcare – raising quality and giving parents more choice*, available at www.gov.uk/government/publications/more-great-childcare-raising-qualityand-giving-parents-more-choice. Accessed June 25, 2016.

Department for Education (DfE) (2014) *Statutory framework for the Early Years Foundation Stage*, DFE-00337-2014, London: DfE.

Department for Work and Pensions (DWP) and Department for Education (DfE) (2011) *A new approach to child poverty: tackling the causes of disadvantage and transforming families' lives*, London: DWP and DfE.

Dickerson, A. and Popli, G. (2012), *Persistent poverty and children's cognitive development: evidence from the Millennium Cohort Study* (CLS Working Paper No. 2012/2), London: Centre for Longitudinal Studies.

Dockrell, J., Sylva, K., Huxford, L. and Roberts, F. (2007) *I Can Early Talk package: an evaluation in two local authorities*, London: I Can.

Drury, R. (2013) How silent is the 'Silent Period' for young bilinguals in early years settings in England?, *European Early Childhood Education Research Journal*, Vol 21 (3): 380–391.

Eisenstadt, N. (2012) Poverty, social disadvantage and young children, in L. Miller and D. Hevey (eds), *Policy issues in the early years*, London: Sage.

Feinstein, L. (2003) Inequality in the early cognitive development of British children in the 1970 cohort, *Economica*, Vol 70: 73–97.

Field, F. (2010) *The foundation years: preventing poor children becoming poor adults. The report of the independent review on poverty and life chances*. London: Cabinet Office.

Formosinho, J. and Figueiredo, I. (2014) Promoting equity in an early years context: the role of participatory educational teams, *European Early Childhood Education Research Journal*, Vol 22 (3): 397–411.

Foster, B. and Norton, P. (2012) Educational equality for Gypsy, Roma and Traveller children and young people in the UK, *The Equal Rights Review*, Vol 8: 85–112.

Furedi, F. (2001) *Paranoid parenting*, London: Penguin.

Gambaro, L., Stewart, K. and Waldfogel, J. (2013) *A question of quality: do children from disadvantaged backgrounds receive lower quality early years education and care in England?* London: Centre for Analysis of Social Exclusion, London School of Economics.

Grayson, H. (2013) *Rapid review of parental engagement and narrowing the gap in attainment for disadvantaged children*, National Foundation for Educational Research and Oxford University Press.

Hansen, K., Joshi, H. and Dex, S. (2010) *Children of the 21st century: the first five years*, The UK Millennium Cohort Study Series (2), Bristol: The Policy Press.

Her Majesty's Government (HMG) (2014) *Child poverty strategy 2014–17*, London: Her Majesty's Stationery Office.

Hirsch, D. (2007) *Chicken and egg: child poverty and educational inequalities*, London: Child Poverty Action Group.

Institute for Fiscal Studies (IFS) (2013) *Children and Working-Age Poverty in Northern Ireland 2010–2020*, London: IFS.

Law, J., Mensah, F., Westrupp, E. and Reilly, S. (2015) *Social disadvantage and early language delay*, Centre of Research Excellence in Child Language, Policy Brief 1.

Levitas, R. (2012) Utopia calling: eradicating child poverty in the United Kingdom and beyond, in A. Minujin and S. Nandy (eds), *Global child poverty and well-being: measurement, concepts, policy and action*, Bristol: The Policy Press.

Love, J.M., Kisker, E.E., Ross, C., Constantine, J., Boller, K., Chazan-Cohen, R., Brady-Smith, C., Fuligni, A.S., Raikes, H., Brooks-Gunn, J., Tarullo, L.B., Schochet, P.Z., Paulsell, D. and Vogel, C. (2005) The effectiveness of the Early Head Start for 3 year old children and their parents: lessons for policy and programs, *Developmental Psychology*, Vol 41: 885–901.

Machin, S. (2006) *Social disadvantage and education experiences*, OECD Social, Employment and Migration Working Papers, No. 32, Paris: OECD Publishing.

MacNaughton, G. (2006) *Shaping early childhood: learners, curriculum and contexts*, Maidenhead: Open University Press.

Marmot, M. (2010) *Fair society, healthy lives: strategic review of health inequalities in England*, available at www.marmotreview.org.uk. Accessed June 25, 2016.

Mathers, S., Ranns, H., Karemaker, A., Moody, A., Sylva, K., Graham, J. and Siraj-Blatchford, I. (2011) *Evaluation of the Graduate Leader Fund: final report*, London: Department for Education.

Mathers, S. and Smees, R. (2014) *Quality and inequality: do three- and four-year-olds in deprived areas experience lower quality early years provision?* London: Nuffield Foundation.

McClelland, M. and Wanless, S. (2015) Introduction to the special issue: self-regulation across different cultural contexts, *Early Education and Development*, Vol 26 (5–6): 609–614.

Melhuish, E.C. (2004) *A literature review of the impact of early years provision upon young children, with emphasis given to children from disadvantaged backgrounds. Report to the comptroller and auditor general*, London: National Audit Office.

Morrison, F.J. (2015) Understanding growth in self-regulation: international contributions, *Early Education and Development*, Vol 26 (5–6): 893–897.

National Audit Office (NAO) (2012) *Delivering the free entitlement to education for three- and four-year-olds*, Report by the Comptroller and Auditor General, London: National Audit Office.

National Children's Bureau (NCB) (2013) *Greater expectations: raising aspirations for our children*, London: NCB.

Nutbrown, C., Hannon, P. and Morgan, A. (2005) *Early literacy work with families: policy, practice and research*, London: Sage.

Ofsted (2014) *Are you ready? Good practice in school readiness*, available at www.ofsted.gov.uk/resources/140074. Accessed June 25, 2016.

Organisation for Economic Co-operation and Development (OECD) (2011) *Doing better for families*, available at www.oecd.org/es/soc/doingbetterforfamilies.html. Accessed June 25, 2016.

Ridge, T. (2011) The everyday costs of poverty in childhood: a review of qualitative research exploring the lives and experiences of low-income children in the UK, *Children and Society*, Vol 25 (1): 73–84.

Rogoff, B. (2003) *The cultural nature of human development*, Oxford: Oxford University Press.

Sabates, R. (2008) *The impact of lifelong learning on poverty reduction: IFLL public value paper*, London: National Institute of Continuing Adult Education.

Sammons, P., Sylva, K. and Melhuish, E. (2002) *EPPE Technical paper 8b: Measuring the impact of pre-school on children's social/behavioural development over the pre-school period*, London: DfES/Institute of Education, University of London.

Save the Children (2013) *Too young to fail*, London: Save the Children.

Schmitt, S.A., McClelland, M.M., Tominey, S.L., and Acock, A.C. (2015) Strengthening school readiness for Head Start children: evaluation of a self-regulation intervention, *Early Childhood Research Quarterly*, 30(A): 20–31.

Simpson, D., Lumsden, E. and McDowall Clark, R. (2015) Neoliberalism, global poverty policy and early childhood education and care: a critique of local uptake in England, *Early Years*, Vol 35 (1): 96–109.

Social Mobility and Child Poverty Commission (2014) *Cracking the code: how schools can improve social mobility*, London: Social Mobility and Child Poverty Commission.

Sylva, K., Melhuish, E., Sammons, P., Siraj-Blatchford, I. and Taggart, B. (2004) *The Effective Provision of Pre-School Education (EPPE) project: final report*. London: Institute of Education.

Tabors, P. (1997) *One child, two languages: a guide for pre-school educators of children learning English as a second language*, Baltimore: Paul Brookes Publishing.

Taguma, M., Litjens, I. and Makowiecki, K. (2012) *Quality matters in early childhood education and care: United Kingdom (England)*, Paris: OECD.

Tallis, R. (2011) *Aping mankind: Neuromania, Darwinitis and the misrepresentation of humanity*, Durham: Acumen.

Urban, M., Vandenbroeck, M., Van Laere, K., Lazzari, A. and Peeters, J. (2011) *Competence requirements in early childhood education and care: final report*, London and Brussels: European Commission, Directorate General for Education and Culture.

Vandenbroeck, M. (2010) Participation in early childhood education and care programmes: equity, diversity and educational disadvantage, in P. Peterson, E. Baker and B. McGaw (eds), *International encyclopedia of education* (3rd ed), Oxford: Elsevier.

Vandenbroeck, M. and Lazzari, A. (2014) Accessibility of early childhood education and care: a state of affairs, *European Early Childhood Education Research Journal*, Vol 22 (3): 327–335.

Wastell, D. and White, S. (2012) Blinded by neuroscience: social policy, the family and the infant brain, *Families, Relationships and Societies*, Vol 1 (3): 397–414.

Wilkin, A., Derrington, C., White, R., Martin, K., Foster, B., Kinder, K. and Rutt, S. (2010) *Improving the outcomes for Gypsy, Roma and Traveller pupils: final report*, Research Report DFE-RR043, London: DfE.

5
TRANSITIONS AND STARTING SCHOOL

Introduction

Children are likely to undergo successive transitions during early childhood, but that from preschool to formal education within primary school is imbued with special significance. Transition into school provides a challenge that, if well-planned and supported, is generally 'a stimulus to growth and development' (OECD 2006). Unfortunately, as the OECD go on to note, if transitions are 'too abrupt and handled without care, they carry . . . the risk of regression and failure (2006: 3).

> Jay and Elliott are brothers born two and a half years apart. Jay's fourth birthday was in early spring and he began school the following September, settling in quickly and making good progress. When he heard all the interesting things Jay was doing, Elliott was keen to go to school too. He started two years later, three weeks after his fourth birthday. Within a very short time Elliott changed his mind about school and told his Mum he didn't want to go any more. He struggled to sit still and became increasingly frustrated at his inability to do the things that were asked of him. Elliott was placed in the lower ability group and began to lose confidence in himself – 'I'm no good at writing' he told his mother. His behaviour in class led to Elliott regularly getting into trouble and he started to acquire a reputation for being disruptive. Privately the teachers compared him to his older brother who was hardworking, responsible and never any trouble.

When children walk through the doors of a classroom, they bring with them a unique bundle of needs, interests and values. The classrooms they enter offer a range of interesting things to do, teachers and other adults to relate to and a curriculum to guide classroom activity. When these interactions go well, the classroom functions as a support system for children to satisfy their needs, explore interests, refine skills, internalise values and develop socially. In such conditions children show strong motivation, active engagement and meaningful learning: the real readiness factors. Things are not always so straightforward however, and classrooms may place too many demands upon children, which they are inexperienced to meet. Young children's experiences will be more positive in conditions where they take part in playful activities full of meaning and can use their own ideas. Children will then not need external incentives and coercion because their engagement and autonomous self-motivation enable them to accept challenges and lead to deep learning.

This chapter examines the circumstances of transition to formal schooling to evaluate factors that impinge on policy, practice and the concept of readiness. Implications of children being admitted to school considerably before the compulsory starting age are discussed as well as the issues of assessment this raises. Peters and Dunlop (2014) suggest that, despite a wealth of research and policy attention, the gap between cultures of preschool and primary school appear remarkably resistant to change. The nature of curriculum and pedagogical provision is examined in an attempt to shed light on why this remains the case. Finally it is important to remember that transition to school does not concern young children alone; it is also a transition for their parents. Successful transitions that support children's well-being and positive learning should include collaboration between family, preschool setting and school, developing a broad and interlinked concept of readiness that builds competencies and preparedness in children, schools and families (UNICEF 2012). This chapter considers perspectives of different stakeholders as they work together to ensure each child experiences a successful transition and a positive start to formal schooling.

Starting school

School entry in the UK is based on age cohorts rather than perceived readiness as in some countries. The age of school entry, as noted in Chapter 1, varies widely across the world. In most of Europe as well as the USA, children are not regarded as ready for school – in other words, ready for formal teaching and learning – until at least 6 years of age. In the UK children are likely to begin in a primary school Reception class at age four. Whereas it used to be the case that children did not start school until the term after their fifth birthday, earlier admittance to school is now exacerbated by the practice of having just one admissions point for Reception in September of each year. Hence some children enter Reception aged almost five, whereas others are only just four years old although no change to provision has been made to allow for this younger intake. The fact that some children are relatively old and others relatively young upon entry into school raises issues for teachers and children alike, but it is the youngest children, beginning school with much fewer life experiences, for whom consequences are most serious.

Beginning school places many demands on young children who have to leave familiar, comforting surroundings and encounter new routines and structure to the day. They must adapt, in a short space of time, to an environment with higher adult–child ratios and very different expectations about how they should conduct themselves. Starting school involves children in responding to changes in identities, roles and relationships as they become pupils and learn social rules and new values associated with being part of an institution. This can provide a positive experience when the challenge fosters resilience in children, helping prepare them for a future of change (Brooker 2008).

It is important to bear in mind that, on starting school, children have already mastered an array of knowledge and skills. Each will have experienced a unique range of previous events and opportunities, some more positive than others, which has shaped the range of skills they are ready to employ and their disposition towards future learning. There is nothing predictable or uniform about the combination of attributes and skills with which any individual child arrives at school and there are substantial differences across children that persist as they get older. This means that transitions will be experienced quite differently by each child within the class.

Transition into primary school poses difficulties for young children when they encounter contrasting or widely differing expectations, approaches and values in the new environment. For many children, the transition and adjustment can be relatively straightforward – new learning may be challenging but a change of environment, friendships, teaching style and activities, whilst demanding, will also be exciting and rewarding. In the main, these are children who share the set of codes, language and cultural resources valued in mainstream education. For children with different codes, languages and cultural resources the transition and adjustment to school may pose more difficult challenges. These children, though very capable in many ways, can find the transition to school extremely difficult because in effect, their readiness for school is measured against a one-size-fits-all model – and many will be found wanting. For example, many children, who speak fluently in their first language and enjoy early literacy activities at home, may be labelled deficient in English. Others, used to a high degree of self-regulation in selecting and carrying out what they want to do, may be seen as hyperactive as they move from an environment that encourages autonomy into one of conformity and teacher-dependency with lack of choice or explanatory discourse.

Diversity of intake

Evidently, the readiness of each child to begin formal learning in school varies widely. As the previous chapter highlighted, the make-up of society in England is extremely complex; there is no such thing as a typical child who experiences a typical range of early childhood experiences. Some four-year-olds will already possess cognitive prerequisites for academic content when they join a Reception class, whereas others will not yet have developed such skills or still be in the process of developing them. Katz (2010) stresses that teachers should not assume because children have not been exposed to skills associated with school readiness at home, they do not have lively minds. She points out that although children may not have been read to or had the opportunity to hold a pencil, this does not mean they lack ability to do so.

Arguably the most important prerequisite is spoken language ability and some children's previous experience may have limited their opportunities to develop appropriate language and cognitive skills. Given the widely accepted link between early language ability and later literacy development (Snow 2006), the potentially negative impact on children's academic achievement is clear. Learning to read and write not only builds on spoken language, but also requires additional skills such as perceptual and spatial development and physical fine motor control. For children who have not yet developed these capabilities, teachers need to scaffold development through appropriate activities related to their interests, such as supporting awareness of syllables and rhyme or providing opportunities for developing fine motor skills. Different children's ability to engage in school-based learning varies widely in the Reception class so each must be treated as an individual whilst at the same time remembering that children's learning is primarily a social activity requiring common goals and shared activities (Goswami 2015).

Children also differ in their social and emotional development with some struggling to pay attention or follow instructions (Aubrey and Ward 2013). As socio-emotional development is strongly linked to cognitive processing, academic progress can be reinforced by adults building children's self-regulation abilities and the executive functions that underpin learning. Children who begin school with weak executive functions are often perceived as badly behaved; consequently teachers respond in a negative manner and as a result children are likely to become resistant to school and schoolwork. By contrast, those with better self-regulation encounter positive feedback from teachers and enjoy school. Relatively small differences at the outset are progressively enlarged over time as young children experience positive or negative feedback loops, resulting in increasingly divergent learning trajectories and a widening achievement gap (Bingham and Whitebread 2012: section 2.4).

It is important that children who are still developing in certain areas are not labelled as deficit but given the opportunity to gain the necessary skills to make progress and reach their potential. Wall et al. (2015) highlight the challenge for pedagogy presented by such a range of starting points and stress that pedagogies must be adapted to the diverse needs of a wide range of children. The diversity of any class of children as they begin formal schooling raises questions in regard to how they are assessed as pupils within a new system, an issue examined later in this chapter.

Age of entry and summer-born children

Children who begin school younger than their peers are particularly liable to have not yet developed underlying skills for formal learning by the start of Reception class. This means that children born in the summer are likely to encounter difficulties due to their relative immaturity. Sykes et al. (2009) suggest that summer-born children may be 'doubly disadvantaged' in that they are both *young* (possibly just having had their fourth birthday) and the *youngest* in their class when they start school. In being admitted a year ahead of statutory school age these children are less likely to have reached levels of cognitive competence required to tackle a curriculum formulated for five-year-olds and may also experience other difficulties in transition.

To cope with the demands of a school day, Reception class children need levels of physical, social and emotional maturity normally expected of five-year-olds so younger children may struggle socially and emotionally to manage new expectations. Sykes et al. (2009) point out that children around the age of four are frequently not ready for the formal environment they encounter in Reception classrooms, including a curriculum not necessarily tailored to their needs as well as situations requiring social and emotional adjustments. There are fewer adults to whom they can relate as well as a greater number of children with whom they must interact. Adapting to a new structure with less support than they are used to or understanding and adhering to new rules may prove particularly difficult. Of course these factors apply to all children beginning school, but older children in the class, being more mature, may not suffer the same degree of stress and anxiety experienced by younger peers. Young children's participation and their positioning as learners is closely linked to their chronological place in a cohort (Payler 2007).

The youngest children's lower levels of maturity in physical, cognitive, social and emotional areas leads to considerable disparity in achievement as those who are more mature at the start of school consistently outperform others (Sharp et al. 2009). English children born in August for example are on average around 25 percentage points less likely to reach the expected level in Key Stage 1 than those born in September of the same year (Crawford et al. 2007). Critical birth months vary – for instance, in Northern Ireland the cut-off point for starting school is reaching age four by July 1, so the youngest children in each class are those born earlier in the year whilst July- and August-born children are the oldest – but the relative age effects are the same. The birthdate phenomenon is persistent and, although becoming less pronounced over time, disparity in scores between the youngest and oldest cohorts in each class remain evident throughout primary and secondary education. Moreover, the knock-on effect in terms of GCSEs means August-born children are less likely to remain in education beyond the age of 16. Additional consequences include potential bullying and a disproportionately high diagnosis of special educational needs – 23 per cent of summer-born children are identified as having SEN compared to 15 per cent of autumn-born and 17 per cent of those born in the spring (Gledhill et al. 2002). Many children are regarded as having learning difficulties or behaviour problems when they are not less able but merely younger and less experienced, but Gledhill and colleagues suggest simple changes to classroom practice can increase teachers' awareness of age effects and so help lessen the incidence of summer-born children diagnosed with SEN. Such measures include arranging the register in order of date of birth or, in two-form entry schools, organising classes according to season of birth.

Children born prematurely may similarly lag behind peers because development tends to be in line with their due date rather than date of birth. In addition, being born earlier than expected may result in them falling into a different age group.

Concerns about adverse impacts for summer-born and premature children entering school so young has led to calls for greater flexibility in admissions systems (Long 2015). The Schools Admissions Code has traditionally taken the view that children's needs should be met through differentiation of the curriculum so they should only be educated out of their normal age group in very limited circumstances. Whilst parents have a right to request part-time attendance for their child, or defer entry until statutory school age, not all parents are aware of this and children who enter school at age five are usually expected to join Year 1 where they immediately encounter a more formalised approach to curriculum. Parents' rights have not extended to being able to insist their child is admitted to a particular age group; that decision is the responsibility of the school admission authority, required to act in the best interests of each child (DfE 2014b).

After reviewing a wide range of international research to determine the extent that attainment and development is affected by children's age relative to their year group, Sharp et al. (2009) conclude that deferring entry for children not yet considered ready for school, or, as happens in some countries, requiring children to repeat a year, does not satisfactorily address age effects. Instead they recommend a focus on ensuring that curriculum and pedagogy are developmentally appropriate for relatively younger children; indeed Rogers and Rose (2007) argue that decisions about school entry systems are inextricably linked to pedagogical and curricular provision.

Curriculum and pedagogy revisited

The age when children begin school appears to be less significant than the quality of provision and educational practices they encounter when they get there. Whilst early educational experience is known to be important, this is not necessarily met by an early start at school. Indeed, unsuitably formal approaches are potentially harmful as instruction-based learning erodes children's own motivation and learning dispositions. EPPE found better practice more likely within nursery schools and classes where children experience informal play-based opportunities for learning, rather than in Reception classes (Sylva et al. 2004). The reason for this lies in different providers' interpretations and approaches to curriculum and pedagogy.

The Reception year in primary school is intended as an integral part of the Early Years Foundation Stage (EYFS). The early learning goals are identified as knowledge, skills and understanding that children should have gained by the *end* of the academic year in which they turn five and the pedagogical approaches to bring this about is made explicit:

> Each area of learning and development must be implemented through planned, purposeful play and through a mix of adult-led and child-initiated activity. Play is essential for children's development, building their confidence as they learn to explore, to think about problems, and relate to others. Children learn by leading their own play, and by taking part in play which

is guided by adults. . . . Practitioners must respond to each child's emerging needs and interests, guiding their development through warm, positive interaction. As children grow older, and as their development allows, it is expected that the balance will gradually shift towards more activities led by adults, to help children prepare for more formal learning, ready for Year 1.

(DfE 2014a: section 1.8)

The emphasis on play-based experience with only gradual introduction to structured learning and formal whole class activities advocated here is not always apparent in Reception classes and in actuality practice frequently resembles that at Key Stage 1. The early years curriculum has become distorted by undue emphasis on literacy and numeracy; literacy experiences in particular are liable to entail inappropriate formal teaching methods due to downward pressure from the phonics check at KS1. This erodes opportunities for a broader range of activities to nurture characteristics of effective early learning.

The UK is not alone in assigning a preparatory stage spanning preschool and school provision. Many countries have transition classes labelled with a range of names, such as kindergarten class, reception class or preschool class, working with a common curriculum framework to enable smooth transitions across different systems. Familiar curricular structures are intended to bridge the institutional divide for children by ensuring continuity in the year before official school entry. In the UK, continuation of the Early Years Foundation Stage into Reception year in England is echoed by the Scottish Early Level of the *Curriculum for Excellence 3–18*, applying to Nursery and Primary One. In Wales the Foundation Phase, covering ages three to seven, demonstrates official recognition that active learning is important beyond the first year of statutory schooling and although beginning school at a younger age than any other country, the Northern Irish Early Years Strategy covers children to the end of Year 2 (age six years). An international perspective reveals many different responses to shared concerns in respect of transition between preschool and school but different philosophies and teaching methods between the two systems means the institutional divide remains problematic (Einarsdottir et al. 2008).

This makes it particularly difficult for Reception teachers who must try to maintain balance between the playful interactions and open-ended activity at the root of effective teaching in the Early Years Foundation Stage and the downward push of expectations from further up the school and from some parents. Teachers are frequently judged on how their class performs, so if KS1 colleagues prioritise literacy and numeracy targets and school-based routines then this pressure is likely to translate into a more didactic approach to teaching. Ofsted (2015a), however, striving to dispel 'the recurring myth' that teaching and play are separate, disconnected endeavours, state that a fixed, traditional view of teaching will not suffice. Their definition of teaching in the early years echoes the pedagogical approach outlined in the EYFS.

Teaching should not be taken to imply a 'top down' or formal way of working. It is a broad term which covers the many different ways in which adults help young children learn. It includes their interactions with children during planned and child-initiated activities: communicating and modelling language, showing, explaining, demonstrating, exploring ideas, encouraging, questioning, recalling, providing a narrative for what they are doing, facilitating and setting challenges. It takes account of the equipment they provide and the attention to the physical environment as well as the structure and routines of the day that establish expectations. Integral to teaching is how practitioners assess what children know, understand and can do as well as take account of their interests and dispositions to learning (characteristics of effective learning), and use this information to plan children's next steps in learning and monitor their practice.

(Ofsted, 2015b)

The approach to teaching outlined here is clearly quite different to the narrow focus on abstract, formal learning too often visible in Reception classrooms (TACTYC 2011). Despite the fact that Reception is part of the Early Years Foundation Stage, external requirements to focus on phonics and other formal outcomes restrict the learning opportunities available in order to prepare for school practices. Adams et al. (2004) found a considerable gap between rhetoric and practice in many Reception classes where children are expected to engage in formal processes at the expense of active learning.

A 'preparation for school' model offers education ministries the security of children entering primary school already prepared for reading and writing, and able to conform to many classroom routines. Bingham and Whitebread (2012: section 2.3) suggest Governments may, purposely or otherwise, interpret key research studies from a traditional perspective as supportive of structured approaches to curriculum and learning. An example is EPPE's promotion of instructive learning environments and clear learning objectives to extend children's learning (Siraj-Blatchford et al. 2002). Although the findings are not remotely at odds with the pedagogical approach of social constructivism, a huge divide has appeared in the *interpretation* of such recommendations. Whereas educationalists within the social constructivist approach believe it is primarily through children's increased agency and the pursuit of more holistic aims that deep learning occurs, others have thought the safest option is to transfer curriculum downwards from primary school in terms of subject areas and pedagogical approaches. Such pre-primary approaches to the early years period are found in England, the US, Australia, Canada, France, Ireland and parts of the Netherlands (OECD 2006). As a consequence, natural learning strategies of young children – play, exploration of the outdoors and freedom of movement, social interaction and discussion with others within the classroom – are not always encouraged. Structural issues also impact; class ratios in England normally exceed 20 children per teacher in Reception classes, sometimes within small-sized classrooms with limited access to the outdoors. In such circumstances it can be difficult for teachers to sustain an inter-relational, playful curriculum where young children are free to pursue their own interests so it may feel safer to deliver a prescriptive curriculum.

Even when Reception classes succeed in maintaining a play-based curriculum, the move to Year 1 is likely to bring expectations that children will spend a considerable portion of each day sitting still and listening to the teacher. For young children, discontinuities in terms of pedagogical approach are a major concern, perceived by them in terms of 'hard work', less choice and the boredom of being expected to sit still for long periods of time (Sanders et al. 2005). Continuity of experience is just as important at this stage as when children first begin school, but because it takes place within the same setting, the significance of the move may be missed. Abrupt changes in expectations and daily experience can make transition from Reception to Y1 more difficult than the start of school, especially for younger, less mature children and those who speak English as a second language. Children may struggle to adapt to subject-based teaching with limited choice and play and Sanders et al. (2005) suggest that the skills of independent learning that children acquire during the Early Years Foundation Stage are not always capitalised on in Year 1.

Implications of formalised approaches within the first years of school

Direct teaching of academic skills may seem to offer a simple shortcut to achievement but formal teaching of skills is completely at variance with research evidence. It has been shown, for example, that by age eleven there is no difference in reading ability between New Zealand children, who begin learning to read at seven years old, and children in England who start at least two years earlier (Suggate 2007). Where there is a difference is in children's disposition towards reading. Suggate explains this by reference to the 'Luke effect' whereby reading skills develop much quicker and more effectively in older children. As a result English children tend to be much less keen to read, demonstrating poorer comprehension skills than those who start sufficiently mature to tackle abstract learning.

An emphasis on formal literacy and numeracy targets is counterproductive because it comes at the expense of children's own personal, social and emotional development. The fact that children at age five have not yet developed social skills for learning has been suggested as the reason British children are more likely to be 'off task', falling behind their Japanese counterparts who start school a whole year later (Whitburn 2000). In the early stages of education, cognitive and intellectual development is more important than academic learning. Opportunities to pursue their own enquiries give children the chance to develop the communication skills and physical and social competences that underpin later formal learning. Activities that challenge children enable them to make choices and support decision-making; being able to make mistakes and learn from them encourages understanding that there are often different ways of arriving at an answer and develops children's confidence in themselves as competent learners. All these are necessary foundations for later success and should be part of effective learning and teaching through early years and primary schooling. Children who do not have the opportunity to develop the skills needed to regulate their own learning and meet the demands of the curriculum are likely to be left behind at KS1.

The implications of inappropriate teaching methods in the early years of education are grave because they not only affect children's current participation but have long-term consequences for their future. Research from the Head Start programme in the US (Schweinhart et al. 2005) tracked children who experienced different types of early years provision from preschool through to adulthood. Whilst formal, teacher-led direct instruction seemed to bring some children initial advantages in early reading and numeracy, in the long term participants became disaffected with learning. Those who had been in social constructivist learning environments showed significantly more positive results and by age 23 were eight times less likely to need treatment for psychological or emotional disturbances and three times less likely to be arrested for committing a crime. It seems that social problems arise when policy and curriculum directives fail to recognise that early education should be about the whole child; direct instruction does not *cause* social problems, but depriving children of the opportunity to develop socially is an unintended side effect.

Falling behind from the start

Many educators feel that certain Early Learning Goals in communication, language and literacy and problem solving, reasoning and numeracy are pitched at too demanding a level and that focus on these takes precedence over children's development of skills for learning. House (2012) suggests that practitioners are placed in a quite 'intolerable' situation by being made responsible for exposing young children to learning experiences they believe to be harmful. In particular, there are concerns about numeracy and writing where requirements are inappropriately demanding and formal for most children in the age group; Early Years Foundation Stage Profile scores (DfE 2015a) show that writing goals are generally more challenging than other goals, especially for boys. Norbury et al. (2016) suggest current targets set for children in their first year at school are not developmentally appropriate and call for academic targets to reflect developmental capacity. They point out that very young children starting school have relatively immature language and behaviour skills and many are not yet ready to meet the academic and social demands of the classroom.

By setting goals that are too demanding, children can easily become labelled as behind in their development. This applies particularly to boys, bilingual children and disadvantaged children as well as summer-borns who are much less likely to achieve writing goals by Year 1. Too strong a focus on formal and, for many children, unachievable goals, has a tendency to direct attention to children's deficits rather than their strengths and capabilities. This sets up an effect of teacher expectancy that follows a child throughout their schooling. It is known for instance that the youngest children are far more likely than their peers to be placed in low-ability groups (Sykes et al. 2009). Not only learning goals but restrictions of the classroom and inappropriate provision for learning can also negatively affect teachers' perceptions of children. Expectations that children should sit down at tables and formally record their 'work' do not match their natural propensity for active exploration and independent discovery, leading many to be misjudged and underestimated. Maynard et al. (2013) found that observing child-initiated play in outdoor spaces could diminish teachers' view of children as underachieving. Maynard's research took place in Wales where the Foundation Phase framework (DCELLS 2008) advocates an experiential, play-based approach to learning for children up to age seven. Nonetheless the curriculum takes a developmental approach whereby teachers expect to move children along a learning continuum and many teachers recognised that this expectation that children 'should' be able to achieve certain things within the classroom had shaped their perceptions of certain children as 'underachieving'. Maynard and colleagues conclude that child-initiated activity in natural outdoor spaces provides children with the opportunity to reconstruct and reposition themselves as competent children rather than underachieving pupils (p. 223).

The fact that inappropriate environments, practice and expectations can result in a deficit view of those not meeting expected developmental markers and learning goals points to the critical role that assessment plays in young children's start at school.

Assessment

In the first years of schooling there are huge differences in children's individual zones of proximal development (Vygotsky 1978) affecting their ability to benefit from learning opportunities proffered. This makes accurate assessment of children's starting points challenging but essential. Ofsted's study of preparation for school showed that, whilst completing accurate assessments of children's starting points was common to all successful settings, it is of particular importance in areas of high deprivation where children often arrive with learning or developmental delays (Ofsted 2014). As part of transition, teachers are eager to build up a detailed picture of each child so as to plan suitable programmes and address any gaps that could impede progress. Nevertheless the rationale for early years assessment needs careful consideration if it is to promote and protect learning (Carr 2001). Assessment should inform the learning experiences offered to individual children. In Scandinavian countries for example, there is no equivalent of formal skills assessment as practised in the UK but emphasis is placed instead on children's socialisation and development of self-image. In England, use of assessment data for the purpose of school accountability creates tensions for teachers pressed into 'playing the assessment game' through mediating policy expectations at the same time as providing children with the experiences they need developmentally (Basford and Bath 2014). If assessment is to be effective then it must be responsive to children's individual needs and backgrounds, acknowledge their experiences in the home and be culturally sensitive. It must also take place over a period of time, recognising that children's abilities vary across different contexts and with different people.

Formal skills assessment has particular implications for children with special educational needs who are likely to learn differently from neuro-typically developing children. One-size-fits-all models cannot be expected to produce meaningful data about children with specific learning difficulties and any attempt to bring about objective, standardised scores for national comparison, even if desirable, could never succeed. Indeed the very concept of standardisation and objectivity is misguided for *all* young children and the focus should be on processes of learning rather than curricular content. Learning in the early years is individualised and idiosyncratic so assessment should likewise be individualised and qualitative, enabling children to value their own achievements rather than being compared to others. Standardised measures of achievement are necessarily at odds with the principle of the 'unique child' endorsed in the EYFS.

It is important to distinguish between assessment – necessary to gauge children's starting points, interests and capabilities – and testing. The Cambridge Primary Review (CPR 2010) points out the 'widespread assumption that "assessment" and "testing" are synonymous . . . is far from true' (p. 30) and asserts that English children are among the most tested in the world. Subjecting young children to very early, formalised testing is part of what Smith (2016) identifies as a global testing culture in which tests have become closely tied to accountability measures and synonymous with perceived educational quality. Smith argues that when testing is normalised and embedded in the culture as a legitimate policy lever it becomes less open to reflection. Whereas testing for assessment can be formative or summative to support progress, because testing for the purpose of accountability is widely disseminated and allows for comparisons between schools, it is liable to be evaluative and punitive (Smith 2014). This shifts the high stakes from pupil to teacher as educators become responsible for children's performance and, amongst other consequences, it encourages teaching to the test and initial underestimation of children's abilities in order to demonstrate later learning gains (DfE 2015b).

Early Years Foundation Stage Profile

The Early Years Foundation Stage Profile (EYFSP) was introduced to provide a uniform assessment scheme for children in their first year of school, to be completed in the summer term of the Reception year. Intended as an aid to transition by informing dialogue between Reception and Year 1 teachers and assisting planning, the EYFSP may eventually be phased out as the government seeks to replace it with some form of Baseline Assessment scheme.

First introduced in 2003, the Profile evolved over time. Although the number of measures were significantly reduced in 2012 to simplify an excessive burden of assessment, concerns remain about inappropriately demanding expectations (e.g. House 2012; Norbury et al. 2016) and the likelihood of these to skew provision in the first year of school. Children's rates of progress vary considerably so assessment is based on teacher observations throughout the year, judging whether children are 'emerging', 'expected' or 'exceeding' 17 early learning goals (ELGs) in the three prime areas of learning as well as specific areas of maths, literacy, understanding the world and expressive arts and design. Children should be able to consistently and independently demonstrate the identified ELGs and are deemed to have reached a good level of development if they achieve at least the expected level in each of the prime areas plus literacy and numeracy. The EYFSP also requires teachers to describe children's development in terms of the characteristics of effective learning – playing and exploring, active learning, creating and thinking critically – and to share these with parents and Year 1 teachers, although no numerical score is attributed to these.

In 2012 expectations for the EYFSP were moved substantially upwards in the areas of literacy and numeracy. Expectations for four- to five-year-old children include calculations using numbers up to 20 and reading and writing in sentences – academic skills formerly considered more suitable to KS1. Unsurprisingly only 66 per cent of children assessed at the end of the EYFS were judged to have reached a good level of development (DfE 2015a). Rather than judging children as 'failing' at such a young age, questions must be asked about the appropriateness and suitability of the assessment criteria. Inappropriate and unrealistic expectations distort and narrow the curriculum experienced by children, damaging their confidence and motivation. Bradbury (2014) points out that England's use of statutory assessment for this age group is unique within the UK and other regions use less formal methods of assessment that she suggests are more suitable alternatives.

There are evidently serious consequences when substantial numbers of young children are labelled as failing at age five when they have simply not yet finished this important stage of development. Children can easily become stereotyped if teachers' perceptions of lower ability lead them to underestimate certain pupils. It also raises worries for parents, many of whom will have little knowledge of how the profile works, to hear that their child is judged to have not reached a good level of development. Furthermore, when almost half of all children do not achieve EYFSP expectations at the end of Reception there are significant implications for Year 1 teachers who must carefully monitor children's progress and learning needs rather than rush them into the National Curriculum. These are problems that cannot be solved by testing children, nor by more formalised and directed teaching, and the EYFSP has been called 'fundamentally flawed' (House 2012).

Baseline Assessment

Despite concerns about the EYFSP, a pedagogical rationale was made in terms of supporting continuity for children's learning between the end of Early Years Foundation Stage and beginning of Key Stage 1; plans to introduce a Baseline Assessment (BLA) from September 2016 made no such claims. The purpose of BLA had nothing to do with the interests of young children and would have been solely an accountability measure for primary schools when the first cohort of pupils reached the end of Key Stage 2 in 2022. Schools were encouraged to sign up to one of the commercial schemes approved by the Department for Education but strong opposition from leading education experts and teaching unions, combined with concerns about lack of comparability between different schemes, led to plans being dropped.

Baseline Assessments were intended to be completed within the first six weeks of Reception with significant implications for young children's well-being and smooth transition at this sensitive time. Nor would BLA have provided helpful information for teachers in getting to know their class as young children do not demonstrate their full knowledge, understanding and capabilities to unfamiliar adults in new and unknown surroundings. Four-year-olds' ability is not fixed so BLA would not have provided valid or reliable information about children's starting points or capture the complexity of individual learning. Future attempts to introduce some alternative form of assessment will need to take all this into account, building on observation over time and within a range of contexts. Other important factors include how early assessment can allow for different socio-economic, linguistic and cultural groups as well as taking account of children's age at time of assessment; otherwise there is potential for misdiagnosis of special educational needs amongst younger children, disadvantaged children and those from minority ethnic backgrounds. Whilst measures to assess young children's capabilities are intended to support their life chances, the predictive value of such assessment is weak as future attainment cannot be projected in a linear fashion from what four-year-olds 'know' at the beginning of school. Perceived benefits cannot compensate for the potentially damaging effects. It is particularly important to separate out teachers' usual observation and tracking of children's learning and progress from any school accountability measures so that official expectations do not lead to a narrow focus on outcomes (see *Assessing school readiness* in Chapter 1).

Year 1 phonics screening check

The teaching of reading has been a key focus of the standards agenda for past and current governments over many years. During initial development of the EYFS the then Labour government commissioned an independent review of the subject (Rose 2006), and official guidelines for practice have continued to be shaped by its recommendations. Although stating that reading involves much more than decoding words on a page and emphasising the importance of a broad and rich language curriculum, the Rose Review laid particular emphasis on synthetic phonics. The change in pedagogy brought about by this approach has been controversial as it contradicts an expansive body of research over several decades (Wyse and Styles 2007). Nonetheless official promotion of synthetic phonics has continued and a Phonics Screening Check (PSC) was introduced in 2012 'to confirm whether or not children have learned phonic decoding to an age-appropriate standard' (STA, 2012: 5).

Criticism of the PSC focuses on two main issues, namely arguments about prioritising synthetic phonics as the favoured means for teaching reading and concern about the distorting effect that downward pressure exerts on early years literary practices. Whilst phonological awareness is clearly important for reading success – and teachers have always made use of a variety of phonemic approaches in supporting young readers – direct instruction is not necessarily the best way to acquire this (Snow 2006). The advised method schools are required to put in place however, is explicit, sequential teaching of phonemes (sounds) in connection with graphemes (letters) that children must then blend together to form words. This approach rests on the assumption that reading is essentially a code that children can be taught to crack as a mechanical exercise, a perspective exemplified by numerous 'pseudo words' (nonsense words with predictable spelling but no meaning, such as *veep* or *bim*) included in the PSC. It is asserted that these provide a means of determining whether children can accurately apply rules of phonics by 'reading' such 'words' accurately but critics argue that it simply encourages reading without understanding. Davis (2013) emphasises that decoding is not reading, but only one of many strategies that children may use, and claims that the PSC has a serious impact on conceptions of what reading 'really is'.

The phonics check has had consequences for literacy practices in the early years, despite the fact that Wyse and Goswami's analysis of the Rose Review (2008) could find no reliable empirical evidence to support a synthetic phonics approach as the best route to reading success. Wyse and Goswami stress that phonics must be con-textualised, not presented in isolation, an approach consistent with good early years practice. The National Curriculum, by contrast, emphasises application of phonic knowledge and skills 'as the route to decode words' and actively discourages use of other strategies, such as contextual or semantic cues to work out words. This expec-tation shapes literary provision through adoption of decontextualised approaches that disregard meaning but train children to pass the test, for instance through use of flashcards featuring pseudo words in preparation for the unnatural activity of reading non-words. There is also a downward push into the Early Years Foundation Stage with formal introduction of phonemes early so that children have sufficient time to learn all that is prescribed before the PSC at the end of Year 1. Such testing-focused preparatory activities interfere with a rich language curriculum emphasising reading for pleasure and purpose, calling into question the effectiveness of phonics screening as a means to improve reading standards. Although the government points to success, with yearly increase in the percentage of children meeting the expected measure (DfE 2015a), this can be explained by continuing emphasis on preparing children for the test rather than genuine improvement in reading. Pressure on schools to pass children means teachers are also likely to give them the benefit of the doubt to ensure they meet the threshold (Law and King 2014).

Like the Early Years Foundation Stage Profile and Baseline Assessment, phonics screening is not tied to a child's age but administered at a particular time of the school year. Therefore considerable disparity must be expected between performance of children aged 6.9 in comparison to those who are still only 5.9. Officially 'no attempt has been made to account for the age of the child' because 'the government has high expectations for all children' (STA 2012: 9) but Law and King's analysis of results (2014: 7) clearly demonstrates how performance drops steadily for each month of birth from September (79 per cent) through to August (61 per cent).

The damaging effects of such unfair age discrimination has led Sharp et al. (2009) to call for age-standardised assessment. Such a move could go some way towards forestalling some of the more damaging effects of high-stakes assessment but, whilst assessment is so strongly tied to accountability measures rather than focused on children's learning, the underlying purpose of assessing young children remains deeply flawed. Subsequent consequences for children's learning experiences are serious – as Anning observed almost two decades ago 'what research does show is that early childhood teachers change what and how they teach when assessment tools make them accountable for what children learn' (1998: 311). Increasing emphasis on readiness thus shapes teachers' approach to pedagogy and curriculum to meet the expectations apparent in early years assessments.

Building partnerships for transition

In their study of transition from the Early Years Foundation Stage to KS1, Sanders et al. (2005) suggest that transition should be viewed as a process rather than an event; this is a useful perspective that helps keep in mind that the process is a lengthy one, extending from preschool, throughout Reception year and into Year 1. Ecological models of transition recognise that many people will contribute to enabling a smooth and positive transition (Fabian and Dunlop 2007) and their interaction ensures children's individual needs, capabilities and interests are supported from the start. Whilst schools and early years settings will have developed their own transition strategies, building the necessary relationships can be challenging in practice and requires respect for expertise across different areas of children's lives. Preschool practitioners and teachers need to collaborate to develop understanding of children's particular characteristics and backgrounds, but beyond information sharing they also have a great deal of professional knowledge to share. There is frequently an uneven distribution of power in these relationships and, when this is the case, school practices are likely to be given precedence (Peters and Dunlop 2014). It is important for all educators to cross boundaries and find ways to overcome practical constraints to support transition, for instance through building shared understandings of curriculum, pedagogy and how children learn. Joint CPD opportunities are a valuable way to promote this. This is advocated by the Scottish Transitions Advisory Group which recommends every preschool and primary setting should appoint a designated transitions coordinator to support opportunities for dialogue and build bridges (Learning and Teaching Scotland 2010).

Collaboration with parents is an equally crucial aspect of transition to ensure the process is not a disruptive experience for young children. Drawing on parents' expert knowledge of their child enables teachers to build up a detailed picture of each individual, with parents and carers regarded as partners in their children's education. All parents have aspirations for their children when starting school but it is not always easy to negotiate dominant school systems and a recent report indicated that 71 per cent of parents are anxious about the transition and feel they need more information and support (PACEY 2013). To counteract this, PACEY launched a *Starting School Together* project with parents' guides and resources to support children and families in the months before starting school and across the first terms. Project coordinators promote partnership between families, preschool settings and primary schools providing a good model for wider adoption. In particular families with a range of complex support needs are less likely to have positive relationships with schools (Dockett et al. 2011). Parents can feel vulnerable and deskilled at a time of transition so families' circumstances should be acknowledged with schools demonstrating responsiveness to children's diverse needs in such a way as to build on families' strengths. Transition can be especially complex for children with disabilities or special educational needs and parents can struggle to advocate for their child's individual needs, finding it difficult to hold out against attempts to fit the child into school systems (Peters and Dunlop 2014).

Even when family engagement is straightforward and positive, many parents do not know what to expect when their child begins school or moves on from the Reception year (Sanders et al. 2005). Parents may have limited understanding of appropriate pedagogical experiences leading them to hold unrealistic expectations for their children once they are in school. They may expect children to be writing their name or doing sums and parents' recognition of underlying skills and prerequisites for such formal activities cannot be assumed. Such expectations can be exacerbated by feedback from assessments which alter home–school relationships as testing increasingly becomes the focus of parent–teacher relations, shaping their interactions (Smith 2014). Assessment in the early years of school may affect parents' understanding of what is important for their child's learning, for instance Baseline Assessment is likely to make them anxious about their child's performance at a critical time when the focus should be on settling children into school so they feel secure and comfortable enough to learn effectively. Similarly phonics screening could encourage parents to focus inappropriately on emphasising individual phonemes and sounds rather than on conversation and sharing books together. Murray (2015) suggests that this sort of schoolification is beginning to intrude on family life and that too narrow an interpretation of the home learning environment brings about a 'family pedagogy' that affects parent–child interactions. Good transition practices welcome and encourage parental engagement by valuing the important learning that takes place in informal contexts of family life, reinforcing rather than replicating school learning.

Children's role in partnership working is often overlooked (McDowall Clark 2013) and recognition of them as active agents in the changes affecting their lives is an important element of the transition process. Dockett and Perry (2002) point out how children's own perspectives are frequently missing from discussion about transition and the importance children place on relationships is paid little regard beyond a set of social skills to be mastered before starting school. Elsewhere they demonstrate the positive results of involving young children in planning and organisation of the transition to primary school, highlighting how their perspectives help teachers identify aspects of children's experiences that might otherwise escape their notice (Perry and Dockett 2011). Children's participation is a crucial aspect of transition processes and can help them build up what Dunlop has called 'transition capital' (2007: 165).

Conclusion

Effective connections between early years provision and primary schools can be difficult to achieve on account of the very different traditions from which each has arisen (Kaga 2008). Whilst schools have been an established part of the education system since the nineteenth century, ECEC is relatively recent and a much less uniform phenomenon. This gives rise to quite different features and results in a different emphasis within the two sectors. Educators from the early childhood tradition value holistic development, activity-based pedagogy and learning processes, in contrast to the emphasis placed on academic learning, formal teaching and learning outcomes within the school system. Such expectations may result in a measure of rigidity that can make adjustment to the demands of schooling particularly difficult for some children and distort perceptions of their readiness.

Transition to schooling raises issues for everyone concerned with young children's well-being and learning, so mutually respectful partnerships between families, preschool provision and schools are evidently crucial to ensure a sound basis for smooth transitions. Settings need to develop a shared collective response built on localised, mutual understandings and parents are integral to this (Ofsted 2014). Despite good intentions on all sides, the power of external expectations can result in attempts to fit young children into the requirements of school and curriculum rather than the other way round. Summer-born and other vulnerable children have a particularly demanding time and, though it is predictable and normal for younger children not to reach an arbitrary, average standard, they are too often perceived as failing, a label that can remain throughout school life.

Over the past decade moves towards increased assessment and formal testing have impacted on transition processes with unhelpful consequences for relationships between teachers, preschool practitioners and parents. Such demands downplay and disregard teachers' professional knowledge (Bradbury 2014) in favour of standardised data gathering that tells us little about the reality of young children's varied approaches to learning or what they already know and can do. Rather than informing planning to support further learning, this encourages teaching to meet assessment targets and is likely to obscure and interfere with the actions schools can take to be ready for children.

A plethora of research evidence and examples from other countries demonstrates that the foundation for children's academic success lies in provision of appropriate learning environments that build on children's interests, enabling them to become confident, autonomous learners. Warm, respectful relationships with teachers who support independent enquiry rather than attempting to control outcomes develops children's intrinsic motivation to tackle new challenges with sustained, focused attention and engenders positive dispositions towards learning (Katz 1993). The current teacher-led, subject-focussed KS1 curriculum, however, is seen by many early years educationalists as fixed, with children being required to fit into it as it stands with no room for compromise.

Transition to formal learning occurs at different points depending on each schools approach. Although elements of play-based learning may still be apparent in Year 1, this is increasingly overshadowed by curriculum demands that exert downward pressure on the Early Years Foundation Stage. The Cambridge Primary Review (Alexander 2010) suggests that what children need from early schooling opportunities is to continue to learn through informal pedagogies – ideally up until the age of seven – in environments offering rich stimulation and sensitive, supportive adults who know how best to provide for their emotional and cognitive needs. Rather than focusing on testing and assessment, early years education should provide a secure foundation for lifelong learning and effectively engage young children's full potential as learners and citizens. Primary school teachers who tap into children's interests and offer opportunities for meaningful and active engagement can draw on children's autonomous motivation. By reinforcing children's developing skills as they take on the challenges of the National Curriculum, this approach is more likely to lead to deep level learning than formal teaching methods.

References

Adams, S., Alexander, E., Drummond, M. and Moyles, J. (2004) *Inside the Foundation Stage: recreating the reception year: final report*, London: Association of Teachers and Lecturers.

Alexander, R. (2010) *Children, their world, their education: final report and recommendations of the Cambridge Primary Review*, London: Routledge.

Anning, A. (1998) Appropriateness or effectiveness in the early childhood curriculum in the UK: some research evidence, *International Journal of Early Years Education*, Vol 6 (30): 299–314.

Aubrey, C. and Ward, K. (2013) Early years practitioners' views on early personal, social and emotional development, *Emotional and Behavioural Difficulties*, Vol 18 (4): 435–447.

Basford, J. and Bath, C. (2014) Playing the assessment game: an English early education perspective, *Early Years*, Vol 34 (2): 119–132.

Bingham, S. and Whitebread, D. (2012) *School readiness: a critical review of perspectives and evidence*. Report prepared for TACTYC, available at www.tactyc.org/projects/. Accessed June 25, 2016.

Bradbury, A. (2014) Early childhood assessment: observation, teacher 'knowledge' and the production of attainment data in early years settings, *Comparative Education*, Vol 50 (3): 322–339.

Brooker, L. (2008) *Supporting transitions in the early years*, Maidenhead: Open University Press.

Cambridge Primary Review (CPR) (2010) *Cambridge Primary Review briefings: the final report*, available at www.primaryreview.org.uk. Accessed June 25, 2016.

Carr, M. (2001) *Assessment in early years settings*, London: Sage.

Crawford, C., Dearden, L and Meghir, C. (2007) *When you are born matters: the impact of date of birth on child cognitive outcomes in England*, London: Institute of Fiscal Studies.

Davis, A. (2013) To read or not to read: decoding synthetic phonics, *Impact: Philosophical Perspectives of Education Policy*, Vol 20: 1–38.

Department for Children, Education, Lifelong Learning and Skills (DCELLS) (2008) *Framework for children's learning for 3–7 year olds in Wales*, Cardiff: Welsh Assembly Government.

Department for Education (DfE) (2014a) *Statutory framework for the Early Years Foundation Stage*, DFE-00337-2014, London: DfE.

Department for Education (DfE) (2014b) *Advice on the admission of summer born children*, London: DfE.

Department for Education (DfE) (2015a) *Statistical first release, Early Years Foundation Stage profile results in England*, SFR 36/2015.

Department for Education (DfE) (2015b) *Reception baseline research: results of a randomised controlled trial*, Research Brief, Reference: DFE-RB476.

Dockett, S. and Perry, B. (2002) Who's ready for what? Young children starting school, *Contemporary Issues in Early Childhood*, Vol 3 (1): 67–89.

Dockett, S., Perry, B., Kearney, K., Hampshire, A., Mason, J. and Schmied, V. (2011) *Facilitating children's transition to school from families with complex support needs*, Albury, Australia: Research Institute for Professional Practice, Learning and Education, Charles Sturt University.

Dunlop, A.-W. (2007) Bridging research, policy and practice, in A.-W. Dunlop and H. Fabian (eds), *Informing transitions in the early years: research, policy and practice*, Maidenhead: Open University Press.

Einarsdottir, J., Perry, B. and Dockett, S. (2008) Transition to school practices: comparisons from Iceland and Australia, *Early Years*, Vol 28 (1): 47–60.

Fabian, H. and Dunlop, A.-W. (eds) (2007) *Informing transitions in the early years: research, policy and practice*, London: OUP/McGraw Hill.

Gledhill, J., Ford, T. and Goodman, R. (2002) Does season of birth matter? The relationship between age within the school year (season of birth) and educational difficulties among a representative general population sample of children and adolescents (aged 5–15) in Great Britain, *Research in Education*, Vol 68: 41–47.

Goswami, U. (2015) *Children's cognitive development and learning*, York: Cambridge Primary Review Trust.

House, R. (2012) *A summary of critical commentary on 'Reforming the Early Years Foundation Stage (the EYFS): government response to consultation'*, available at www.tactyc.org.uk/pdfs/Reflection-House/pdf. Accessed June 25, 2016.

Kaga, Y. (2008) *What approaches to linking ECCE and primary education?* UNESCO Policy Brief on Early Childhood, no 44, available at http://unesdoc.unesco.org/images/0017/001799/179934e.pdf. Accessed June 25, 2016.

Katz, L. (1993) *Dispositions: definitions and implications*, Urbana, IL: ERIC Clearing-house on Elementary and Early Childhood Education, University of Illinois at Urbana-Champaign, available at http://files.eric.ed.gov.fulltext/ED360104.pdf. Accessed June 25, 2016.

Katz, L. (2010) STEM in the early years, *Early childhood research and practice*, Fall edition, available at http://ecrp.uiuc.edu/beyond/seed/katz.html. Accessed June 25, 2016.

Law, J. and King, T. (2014) Screening phonics in England: a cause for concern? *The On-line Educational Research Journal*, available at www.oerj.org/View?action=viewPDF&paper=111. Accessed June 25, 2016.

Learning and Teaching Scotland (2010) *Curriculum for excellence: preschool into primary transitions*, Glasgow: Learning and Teaching Scotland.

Long, R. (2015), *Summer-born children: starting school*, House of Commons Briefing Paper no 07272, available at http://researchbriefings.parliament.uk/ResearchBriefing/Summary/CBP-7272. Accessed June 25, 2016.

Maynard, T., Waters, J. and Clement, J. (2013) Child-initiated learning, the outdoor environment and the 'underachieving' child, *Early Years*, Vol 33 (3): 212–225.

McDowall Clark, R. (2013) *Is there room for the child in partnership with parents?* Available at www.tactyc.org.uk/pdfs/Reflection-McDowall-Clark.pdf. Accessed June 25, 2016.

Murray, J. (2015) Early childhood pedagogies: spaces for young children to flourish, *Early Childhood Development and Care*, Vol 185 (11–12): 1715–1732.

Norbury, C. F., Gooch, D., Baird, G., Charman, T., Simonoff, E. and Pickles, A. (2016) Younger children experience lower levels of language competence and academic progress in the first year of school: evidence from a population study, *Journal of Child Psychology and Psychiatry*, Vol 57 (1): 65–73.

Ofsted (2014) *Are you ready? Good practice in school readiness*, available at www.ofsted.gov.uk/resources/140074. Accessed June 25, 2016.

Ofsted (2015a) *Teaching and play in the early years – a balancing act?* Available at: www.ofsted.gov.uk/resources/150085. Accessed June 25, 2016.

Ofsted (2015b) *Early years inspection handbook*, available at www.gov.uk/government/publications/early-years-inspection-handbook-from-september-2015. Accessed June 25, 2016.

Organisation for Economic Co-operation and Development (OECD) (2006) *Starting strong II: early childhood education and care*, Paris: OECD.

Payler, J. (2007) Opening and closing interactive spaces: shaping four-year-old children's participation in two English settings, *Early Years*, Vol 27 (3): 237–254.

Perry, B. and Dockett, S. (2011) 'How 'bout we have a celebration!' Advice from young children on starting school, *European Early Childhood Education Research Journal*, Vol 19 (3): 373–386.

Peters, S. and Dunlop, A.-W. (2014) Editorial, *Early Years*, Vol 34 (4): 323–328.

Professional Association for Childcare and Early Years (PACEY) (2013) *What does 'school ready' really mean?* Available at www.pacey.org.uk/Pacey/media/Website-files/school-ready/School-Ready-Report.pdf. Accessed June 25, 2016.

Rogers, S. and Rose, J. (2007) Ready for reception? The advantages and disadvantages of single-point entry to school, *Early Years*, Vol 27 (1): 47–63.

Rose, J. (2006) *Independent review of the teaching of early reading*, London: DfES.

Sanders, D., White, G., Burge, B., Sharp, C., Eames, A., McCune, R. and Grayson, H. (2005) *A study of the transition from the Foundation Stage to Key Stage 1*, London: National Foundation for Educational Research.

Schweinhart, L.J., Montie, J., Xiang, Z., Barnett, W.S., Belfield, C.R., and Nores, M. (2005) Lifetime effects: the High/Scope Perry Preschool study through age 40. *Monographs of the High/Scope Educational Research Foundation* (14), Ypsilanti, MI: High/Scope Press.

Sharp, C., George, N., Sargent, C., O'Donnell, S. and Heron, M. (2009) *International thematic probe: the influence of relative age on learner attainment and development*, London: QCA/NFER.

Siraj-Blatchford, I., Sylva, K., Muttock, S., Gilden, R. and Bell, D. (2002) *Researching effective pedagogy in the early years (REPEY)*, DfES Research Report 356, London: DfES/HMSO.

Smith, W. (2014) The global transformation towards testing for accountability, *Education Policy Analysis Archives*, Vol 22 (116): 1–29.

Smith, W. (ed) (2016) *The global testing culture: shaping education policy, perceptions and practice*, Oxford: Symposium Books.

Snow, C.E. (2006) What counts as literacy in early childhood? In K. McCartney and D. Phillips (eds), *Blackwell handbook of early childhood development*, Oxford: Blackwell.

Standards and Testing Authority (STA) (2012) *Year One phonics screening check pilot 2011: technical report*, London: Department for Education.

Suggate, S. (2007) Research into early reading instruction and Luke effects in the development of reading, *Journal for Waldorf/Steiner Education*, Vol 11 (2): 17–20.

Sykes, E., Bell, J. and Rodeiro, C. (2009) *Birthdate effects: a review of the literature from 1990–on*, University of Cambridge: Cambridge Assessment.

Sylva, K., Melhuish, E., Sammons, P., Siraj-Blatchford, I. and Taggart, B. (2004) *The Effective Provision of Pre-School Education (EPPE) project: final report*. London: Institute of Education.

TACTYC (2011) *The Early Years Foundation Stage through the daily experiences of children*, Occasional paper No. 1, available at www.tactyc.org.uk/occasional-paper1.pdf. Accessed June 25, 2016.

UNICEF (2012) *School readiness: a conceptual framework*, New York: United Nations Children's Fund.

Vygotsky, L. (1978) *Mind in society*, Cambridge, MA: Harvard University Press.

Wall, S., Litjens, I. and Taguma, M. (2015) *Early childhood education and care pedagogy review: England*, OECD, available at www.oecd.org/unitedkingdom/early-childhood-education-and-care-pedagogy-review-england.pdf. Accessed June 25, 2016.

Whitburn, J. (2000) *Strength in numbers: learning maths in Japan and England*, London: NIESR.

Wyse, D. and Goswami, U. (2008) Synthetic phonics and the teaching of reading, *British Educational Research Journal*, Vol 34 (6): 691–710.

Wyse, D. and Styles, M. (2007) Synthetic phonics and the teaching of reading: the debate surrounding England's 'Rose Report', *Literacy*, Vol 41 (1): 35–42.

6

WHERE TO IN THE FUTURE?

Introduction

This book has considered the question of school readiness from a number of perspectives, including official policy expectations, research about young children's learning and effective pedagogies, how diversity and growing inequalities affect perceptions of individual 'readiness' and the processes involved when young children begin to attend formal schooling. Through investigating these different topics it becomes evident that there is fundamental disagreement in regard to the purposes of early years education, whether young children should be prepared for school and for academic learning and what types of experiences and opportunities can best support future success. To sum up, the debate is between two opposing perspectives. One lays stress on playful pedagogies providing opportunities for young children to develop traits and characteristics necessary for effective lifelong learning. The alternative, conflicting, view prioritises an early start to formal academic teaching to lay the groundwork for literacy and numeracy. These two positions, as they stand, are irreconcilable.

In this final chapter the ideological tensions and dilemmas facing those who work with young children will be considered to help readers find a way through competing perspectives and respond to concerns about the readiness of children to enter Reception classes at a very young age. A conceptual model is proposed that unifies agency and structure, recognising readiness as a state of institutions as much as of individual children (Graue 2006). The evidence base supporting early learning and teaching is reviewed and from this some opportunities and strengths to build on are identified as well as challenges to overcome. Finally a number of questions and points for further discussion are raised. It is hoped that these may engender debate amongst those concerned with the education and well-being of young children and help contribute to greater communication: it is only through dialogue that we can make progress in disentangling the issues.

Towards a dynamic model of readiness

Conflicting viewpoints in the readiness debate tend towards two distinct propositions, presented in terms of preparing young children to be ready for school or else its converse, a call for schools to be made ready for the children who attend. The former is the argument favoured by government and policy-makers as it appears to offer a simple solution to the issue of poor educational outcomes for vulnerable and disadvantaged children (Allen 2011; Ofsted 2014). In contrast, early years teachers, academics in the field and education experts argue that attempting to fit children to the expectations of schools is inappropriate and likely to be counterproductive. The Ready Schools trend (Ritchie et al. 2010) prefers to focus on the readiness of schools by developing provision that matches the ways in which young children learn. This standpoint asserts that emphasising the acquisition of knowledge, without equal consideration of the processes through which young children acquire knowledge, is likely to lead to an ineffective and inefficient educational system.

The controversy is customarily expressed in terms of conflict, suggesting the two notions are mutually exclusive and only one can offer a way forward. In fact, neither provides a complete solution because both premises are too static and pay insufficient attention to children's own agency. Evidently, moves to make children 'school ready', if interpreted in a formal, academic sense, place unacceptable demands on children at an unreasonably young age. But this does not mean that children cannot benefit from opportunities to develop skills and dispositions that make them truly ready to benefit from all that school can offer. On the contrary, this is essential, because 'unreadiness' (Tickell 2011) presents different problems and other dangers. All the same, ready children do not take away the responsibility of schools to also be ready to work from children's own starting points. Ready schools are those prepared for a diverse range of children and able to respond to their varied developmental levels by providing environments that capitalise on the skills young children bring with them. Dahlberg et al. (2013) ask whether schools are prepared for children who have been used to the challenging and co-constructive environments of early childhood settings. Children who are genuinely ready for school are independent, self-motivated and intellectually curious and this may be at odds with the universal, fixed measures of achievement that are assumed by a focus on curriculum outcomes.

The position of 'ready children' and that of 'ready schools' differs in where the problem is located – within children themselves, who must be *made* ready for school, or within schools that are insufficiently prepared for the varying developmental levels and needs of such very young children arriving in Reception classes. Both arguments present only part of the picture because they are one-sided and focused to a substantial extent on identifying inadequacies in the other. An alternative model of readiness is put forward here. This recognises that children and contexts shape each other (Sameroff 2009) so it is the interactions between them that must be the key focal point. I have argued elsewhere (McDowall Clark 2013, 2016) that, whereas it is has been customary to consider children as part of the microsystem(s) of family and school/preschool (Bronfenbrenner 1979), contemporary partnership imperatives have the effect of positioning children at meso level. The mesosystem, made up of the relationships between different microsystems, is impacted on, and in turn impacts upon, the exo- and macrosystems of community, economic forces, social structures and political systems. This ecological perspective informs the model of school readiness proposed here where children are viewed as competent beings and active agents within their communities rather than isolated individuals who come into focus when they begin school. Young children's start at school requires a dynamic relationship between child, family, school and the wider community: in other words it rests on ready *schools*, ready *children* and ready *families* (UNICEF 2012).

This alternative orientation views readiness as a sociocultural construct existing within the intersections of connected systems. It is characterised by the interplay between children, parents, schools, preschools and neighbourhoods and is responsive to the cultural and socio-economic environments in which they are embedded. Readiness emerges from transactions occurring across the boundaries of young children's lives and must acknowledge children's communities, cultural knowledge and interests. As such, readiness cannot be quantified but its elements can be identified as part of a conceptual model (see Figure 6.1). Young children are not passive beings to be turned into pupils by educational establishments working with parents and carers. Children are active subjects, affected by and simultaneously affecting their environments. Readiness therefore cannot be a static concept which is achieved, almost achieved or not yet achieved. It is constantly evolving, as are young children themselves, in a process of interrelated systems linked through continual activity and change.

Early years educationalists are, unsurprisingly, averse to the notion of *ready children*. This is because too often it is used to imply a problem with young children that can be put right by ensuring they are ready for school. Used in this way, readiness is a deficit discourse, discernible behind interventions to make up children's purported shortfalls in line with predetermined expectations. Yet natural distaste for such an approach does not mean adopting a laissez-faire attitude, simply waiting and watching for children to develop to a certain point of maturity. By focusing on readiness as a dynamic process, as illustrated above, we can move away from specified levels of prior knowledge and ability, and instead properly value the actual potential and capabilities that young children bring with them to school. This model respects children's natural learning strategies and the relational foundations that underpin them so that *ready children* can be conceived as those with motivation, disposition and confidence to tackle new challenges.

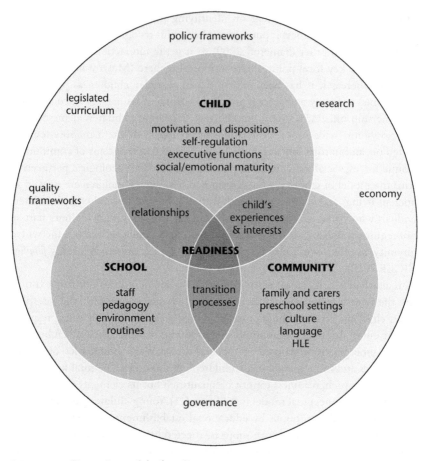

FIGURE 6.1 Dynamic model of readiness

An evidence base to guide practice

Substantial evidence provides a robust rationale for the perspective on readiness set out in this book. A quantity of this has been presented in previous chapters in relation to practice. Many decades of educational research from the UK and across the world provides a convincing case for active, exploratory provision to sustain young children's learning in the early years (Evangelou et al. 2009; Hirsh-Pasek et al. 2009). This enables us to identify the most appropriate environments and experiences to equip children with a sound basis for future academic success and lifelong learning. In addition it indicates the type of skills and abilities that are crucial to enable young children to make sense of the new situations they face at school.

Social justice demands that the UK pays attention to the achievement gap between children from low-income and higher-income families and it is not surprising that policy-makers are concerned to take action to tackle this. But the assumption that direct formal teaching within schools is able to compensate for and ameliorate disadvantage is mistaken and there is strong evidence to show that positive parenting and the home learning environment are more significant factors for children's academic success (Sylva et al. 2010). Arguments in favour of early instruction are not borne out by evidence (Sharp 2002). Although children who are taught literacy and numeracy skills at an early age may show initial gains, this is not sustained in the long term. What is more, the experience can be discouraging and create feelings of failure which are likely to have a negative impact on young children's self-esteem and motivation.

The reason early learning of formal, academic skills does not translate into long-term gains is because formal learning tends to be too abstract for young children's levels of development. For the first six years at a minimum, learning must be active and meaningful. Formal teaching of academic skills at an early age may give an initial impression of knowledge but this is likely to be superficial and not embedded in children's understanding. For example parents often take pride in their toddler's ability to count – and young children are likely to enjoy performing this trick because it gains them adult approval and attention. However, unless that same child consistently recognises three apples and three crayons, understands that four is one more than three and knows how many biscuits are left when one of them is eaten, it must be assumed that they are not a precocious mathematical genius but simply chanting a string of number names. Children need plentiful opportunities to experience concepts in concrete form through active, hands-on activities to embed learning fully. That is why many adults have only a hazy idea of quadratic equations or irregular French verbs; despite having been 'taught' these things in school, the learning was never properly embedded in their understanding.

Open-ended activities are necessary to sustain problem-solving, creativity and decision-making and to foster critical thinking. Learning and teaching that builds on children's innate curiosity and exploratory drive encourages independence, self-management and the opportunity to take responsibility for their own learning. Moving from kindergartens and preschools – environments where they were competent learners – young children need to feel a measure of control within conditions that allow individuals time to learn at their own pace. This is crucial in order to develop self-regulation, that is, children's capacity to manage their own cognition, emotions and behaviour, as without it young children will struggle to acquire academic content (McClelland and Wanless 2015). The ability to self-regulate equips children for long-term educational success and so is the true signs of readiness.

Learning and teaching in the early years is above all interactive and founded in social relationships. Young children need opportunities to engage in sustained collaborative activity alongside peers and with the support of sensitive and responsive teachers. The quality of social interaction underpins communication and language development and so is fundamental to higher-level thinking skills and academic learning. Language is also strongly associated with self-regulation ability and control processes (Bingham and Whitebread 2012: section 2.1) so its importance in early years classrooms is far greater than a narrow focus on literacy would suggest.

None of the factors that evidence demonstrates to be central to young children's lifelong learning operate independently; they interact to provide the contexts and environments that support children's readiness for school. When conditions are right then young children will thrive. This offers the possibility of seamless and continuous transition from preschool programmes to Reception and then into Year 1 rather than the abrupt shift to a completely different social context and set of academic demands that the notion of readiness currently implies. The important issue appears to be not *where* young children's educational needs are met, but whether the types of curriculum they are offered are of high quality, appropriate for their developmental needs and offered through appropriate teaching methods. This presents a number of opportunities and challenges for the future. A number of discussion points related to these are provided within this section with additional critical prompts later in the chapter. It is important to bear in mind however that within an ecological perspective of readiness, all aspects necessarily interact and affect each other.

Opportunities: strengths to build on

The *ready schools* perspective locates the problem of readiness within schools themselves and institutional or organisational factors that result in environments unsuited to young children. In recent years many countries have begun to 're-design' the school entrance phase (CIDREE 2007) and as a result awareness has been growing about the complexities of ensuring appropriate educational provision to meet the particular needs of this age range. Two important aspects of this new focus are increased awareness of carefully planned transition practices and a greater emphasis on partnership with parents and carers. These are approaches that offer strengths to build on and a positive way forward. Yet both also have potential to be hijacked as a means of shaping children to conform to school practices so it is crucial that collaboration is undertaken in a spirit of genuine reciprocity and mutual respect.

Strong and equal partnerships

Transition processes have an important impact on readiness. Differing perspectives and divergent expectations might result in a child being viewed as competent and ready in one context, yet lacking in certain abilities so not at all ready in another (Graue 2006). A shared responsibility for readiness, in its most affirmative and constructive sense, must be built on shared understandings. This can provide a 'strong and equal partnership' between ECEC and statutory schooling (OECD 2006).

Bennett (2013) notes that partnership between preschool settings and primary schools is too often perceived as an operational challenge and so undertaken for expedient purposes to smooth entrance to school. Strategic partnerships can nonetheless lay the groundwork for less instrumental relationships. If sound communication and cooperation exists between microsystems then children's experiences are more likely to be consistent and positive (Bronfenbrenner 1979). Most significantly, partnership provides opportunities for joint reflection on pedagogical beliefs and perceptions of children's learning. In this way, discontinuities that interrupt young children's progressive learning can be reduced or eliminated.

Genuinely equal partnerships as put forward by the OECD (2006) require more than respect and willingness to overcome practical constraints of time and location. Differences in philosophy, ethos and organisation make it difficult to understand each other's sector and too often an unbalanced relationship exists where the priorities of schools predominate (Peters and Dunlop 2014). Bennett (2013) suggests there is insufficient appreciation of what the early years tradition could contribute to the education system. Opportunities for genuine dialogue, rather than mere exchange of information, enable sharing of values and insights and so can lead to greater understanding of others' perspectives. This is important not only when young children first start school but also when they transfer to Y1. The fact that children have already been in school for a year at this point means the significance of the transition is often underestimated. Sanders et al. (2005) suggest that young children's skills of independent learning may be overlooked in Y1 so increasing opportunities for shared dialogue between Early Years Foundation Stage and KS1 teachers can help break down limiting perceptions of children's readiness.

Discussion points:

- What are the challenges that affect cooperation and collaboration between schools and early years settings? Can the philosophy and ethos of each be aligned? How do hierarchies of power impact on these issues and how might they be addressed?
- Sanders et al. (2005) suggest that young children's capacity for independent investigation and learning is not fully appreciated or utilised in Y1 classrooms. How could this situation be improved and how might it affect notions of readiness?

Working with parents

Strong working relationships with parents and carers are central to high quality early years practice (Sylva et al. 2010) and recognition of the crucial role that parents have in their children's education is behind the prevailing emphasis on parenting. Of the five policy levers noted by the OECD to support high-quality early years provision, England has selected *engaging families and communities* as its current policy focus (Taguma et al. 2012). The government set out its plans for involving parents and working in partnership with them in a document *Supporting Families in the Foundation Years* (DfE 2011). Although echoing the government's 'readiness' discourse, identified in Chapter 1, the document is significant in making explicit the need to engage and work with parents. Views of early years education as preparation for later learning, rather than valuable in its own right, means that interventions targeted at families with the aim of changing parents' behaviour and attitudes can have a deficit tone. Nonetheless, the importance now attached to parental partnership lays the groundwork for positive relationships that can support 'ready families' (UNICEF 2012) and parents have strong potential to influence government policy.

Ready families are those where parents are involved in transition as an ongoing process rather than a one-off event (Fabian and Dunlop 2007). This is central to children's successful start in school and the EYFS requirement to work in partnership with parents (DfE 2014) makes collaboration a statutory part of the Reception teacher's role. As with partnerships between primary school and ECEC settings, schools need to find ways to engage with parents from a perspective of respect and equal status rather than through a home school dialogue that assumes that the school is always right (Brooker 2005). Sharing learning and assessment is a positive way to support reciprocal relationships with families and the Ofsted report *Are you ready?* (2014) gives examples of how modern technologies, such as smartphones, can enable schools to encourage parents' contributions to a broader assessment of children's capabilities and learning.

The OECD suggests that England could learn from Nordic countries and New Zealand in developing strategies for working with parents and the wider community (Taguma et al. 2012). There is also much good practice to share in the ECEC sector with its emphasis on engaging with parents in supportive and non-threatening ways. Parents find it more difficult to form relationships once their children move on to school and report 'a more distant and less reciprocal relationship' with their child's Reception teacher (Shields 2009: 237). Shields argues that, although schools work hard at supporting children's transitions, parents' voices are rarely heard in the literature so there can be a gap between what schools provide as part of their 'transition package' and what parents feel they need (p. 245). Similar concerns are echoed at the transfer to Y1 when parents would like more information about transition and the chance to meet their child's new teacher (Sanders et al. 2005). There are opportunities here for schools to form links with families and communities to develop shared perceptions of readiness that arise from children's own backgrounds and interests rather than narrow interpretations with a focus on curricular outcomes. A shared understanding of what it means to be ready for school can help sustain family readiness through transition and the first few years of primary school. It can also help counteract commercial exploitation of parents' natural anxieties to ensure their children get off to a 'good start', evident in umpteen websites, apps and workbooks providing literacy and numeracy activities. Unsuitable academically focused activities lead to 'schoolification' of the home and a 'family pedagogy' (Murray 2015) rather than a focus on social skills, communication, independence and curiosity. They can also lead parents to have inappropriate or too high expectations of their children.

Developing genuine channels of communication and two-way dialogue is especially important when teachers and parents do not share the same educational or cultural backgrounds. A mismatch between school and home in cultural or linguistic terms can make it hard for parents and teachers to communicate and for children to adapt. Teachers are likely to have certain expectations of the role of parents and, with limited understanding of children's home lives, can judge them against these norms. Equally, parents may not understand the school ethos or share the same curricular goals (Brooker 2005). They may favour more formal approaches and be mistrustful of play-based pedagogies. Schools must take the lead in reaching out to establish mutual understanding and respectful relationships with families and communities that can build on the potential of the home for children's learning. This can help mitigate overly narrow interpretations of school readiness and develop provision that is ready for all children.

Discussion points:

- Parents find it more difficult to establish friendly collaboration with schoolteachers than preschool and nursery practitioners. How do schools' assumptions of readiness affect relationships with parents? How can teachers guard against preconceptions of families whose lives lie completely outside their own experiences?
- The Home Learning Environment is recognised as the most crucial factor in young children's development. How can practitioners and teachers support the HLE without undermining or patronising parents? How can they ensure promotion of the HLE does not lead to 'schoolification' of children's home environments?

Pedagogies

When schools adapt to the children they serve, rather than the other way round, learning is child focused instead of beginning with the curriculum and making children fit predetermined goals. Universal measures of children's achievement can easily underestimate children's diverse abilities however, in which case pedagogy becomes dominated by a narrow focus on particular skills. A crucial element of readiness is school's pedagogical approach, as this affects what is seen to be significant, how it is systematically evaluated and how these judgements impact on experiences and opportunities offered to young children as a result.

A recent review of pedagogical approaches comparing England with a number of other countries, including New Zealand and Denmark (Wall et al. 2015), concluded that England has a number of pedagogical strengths. The review appreciates that England is one of the few governments that has commissioned research in its own country to look at which pedagogical practices are found to benefit young children (i.e. Sylva et al. 2004; Siraj-Blatchford et al. 2002). Noted strengths are a curriculum that bridges young children's first year in school and a pedagogical environment emphasising that every child is a unique, competent learner who should be supported to make progress at their own pace. Official recognition of the importance of *process quality* (as opposed to concentrating on structural features) is noticeable in pedagogical guidance that emphasises sustained shared thinking and scaffolding. Wall and colleagues assert that, although the EYFS does not prescribe a pedagogical approach, it sets out parameters that frame pedagogy by recognising the importance of play, appropriate balance between adult-led and child-initiated activity and emphasis on socio-emotional and physical development and creativity. Process quality is also evident in inspection procedures that monitor staff practices and their interactions with children as well as promotion of graduate level qualifications in ECEC.

These pedagogical strengths offer a sound foundation for developing school provision that is fully ready for young children at whatever age they may enter the Reception class. The Cambridge Primary Review asserts that there is no reason why good quality play-based learning cannot be provided in primary schools (Alexander 2010) but, in practice, many Reception classes are overly formal (Adams et al. 2004). The powerful downward pressure of National Curriculum demands and school accountability measures militates against the best pedagogical practices and when children enter school they are likely to experience an environment more closely controlled by adults. What Payler (2007) refers to as 'pedagogic subcultures' create and maintain learning environments so that the curriculum may be differently enacted within school classrooms. Although young children in the Early Years Foundation Stage will experience a range of pedagogical practices depending on their settings, within schools they customarily spend less time on self-initiated activities, are less physically active and spend more time sitting still on the carpet listening to the teacher or at tables performing specific tasks not of their own choosing (TACTYC 2011).

Pedagogy is dependent on an appropriate balance between support and challenge and this requires skilled and sensitive interaction on the part of the teacher. Wall et al. (2015) note that England favours a child-centred approach, leaving the choice of pedagogy to staff, although they also highlight the challenge that diverse populations present and the importance of adapting pedagogies to different needs. The key ingredients of effective pedagogy are outlined in Chapter 3 and these extend its scope and significance far beyond interactions intended to 'teach', as implied in calls to make children ready for school. Social-constructivist pedagogies affirm the importance of the learning environment as an element of pedagogy, defined by Siraj-Blatchford et al. (2002) as inclusive of the concrete learning environment, the family and the community. This pedagogical perspective supports a dynamic model of readiness (as illustrated in Figure 6.1) unifying ready *children*, ready *schools* and ready *families*. From this standpoint, readiness as a characteristic of any given child is refuted. It is constructed instead as 'something contingent and developing rather than … predictive and semi-static' (Graue 2006: 49).

Discussion points:

- Children in early years classes cannot be treated as if they were older pupils. How can teachers of Reception and KS1 classes encourage the development of children's executive functions and self-regulation abilities whilst meeting parents' and schools' curriculum expectations?

- Young children's natural learning strategies are relational, experiential and play based. How can early years classrooms be organised to accommodate active learning and social interaction? What about free-flow access to outdoor spaces?

Tensions and challenges

As has been demonstrated, several positive starting points exist for developing a constructive, shared conception of readiness that builds on strong and equal partnerships from a foundation of research knowledge. At the same time, there are a number of tensions and challenges endangering high-quality early years pedagogy and constraining action. Growing inequality, lack of autonomy and an increasingly assessment-driven curriculum that encourages formal instruction are all sources of tension leading to disconnection between professional knowledge and practices. A better understanding of true readiness may help to create a culture that can mitigate factors putting at risk effective provision for young children in their first years at school.

Inequality

Over the past few years global recession has had a wide impact, but in the main it is children who suffer most and bear the consequences longest (UNICEF 2014). Despite increasing wealth and living standards in Britain as a whole, millions of young children's lives remain blighted by poverty and disadvantage. During the 1990s, an increase in incomes at the top of the scale, with very little change for poorer families, led to increased levels of inequality (Eisenstadt 2012). Currently the same situation appears to be recurring, reversing progress made in the first decade of the twenty-first century. The consequences of disadvantage and social exclusion for children's long-term well-being are discussed in Chapter 4. The National Children's Bureau (2013) asserts that, far from improving over time, the inequality that existed fifty years ago still persists and that unequal childhoods have become a permanent feature of our nation. Ball (2013) echoes the same sentiment in highlighting stark inequalities within the education system. He argues that despite ongoing reforms, the relationship between opportunity, achievement and social class remains stubbornly entrenched and is reproduced by policy.

The long-term consequences of inequality for young children have been recognised in several official reports and reviews. The Field Report (2010) on poverty and life chances noted 'life's race is already determined for most poor children before they even begin their first day at school' (p. 11). The case for tackling the consequences of inequality for health and well-being was similarly argued in the Marmot Review (2010). Nonetheless, few inroads have been made in confronting the realities of social inequalities. On the contrary, although it is generally accepted that social investment is necessary to tackle poverty and disadvantage (OECD 2011), cuts in welfare provision and services have exacerbated problems. Current government policy lays an emphasis on parenting as opposed to improving the circumstances in which families in poverty find themselves (Mathers et al. 2014). This focus means that ensuring school readiness has become widely accepted as the key policy instrument for tackling inequality.

One result of readiness as the means of addressing inequality and disadvantage is that early intervention programmes largely concentrate effort on young children's cognitive performance. Assessments and learning goals mean practitioners' thinking, interaction and communication with young children is increasingly shaped by this agenda (Simpson et al. 2015). Consequently, there is a very real danger that investment in early intervention measures will be ineffectual due to directing attention to the wrong objectives. The achievement gap between disadvantaged children and their more affluent peers can best be reduced by focusing on social skills, language, self-regulation abilities and motivation, but high-quality provision can only go so far. There are deep structural inequalities that educational intervention alone cannot combat.

A curriculum-focused readiness agenda is based on standardised measures of hypothetical ability but, regardless of the age for school entry, children will vary considerably in their social, emotional and intellectual skills when they arrive in Reception classes. Young children from ethnic minorities and low-income families are particularly affected by assumptions of cultural uniformity that position them as 'unready'. Conceptual and pragmatic changes are needed to enhance inclusiveness and complement the natural learning capacities of *all* young children to enable children to fulfil their potential. Ball (2013) argues that the relationship between education and background is complex and we need to move away from the idea that there is a necessary relationship between social circumstances and something called ability. A corollary of this argument is that the relationship between readiness and background is also unpredictable. Notions of readiness that presume a fixed yardstick of physical, intellectual, and social development treat the child as 'an object of normalisation' (Dahlberg et al. 2013: 13) and, despite the EYFS emphasis on 'the unique child', largely attempt to fit young children to white, middle-class norms.

Under the Labour government (1997–2010), child poverty became the target of widespread reform, falling more in the UK than in any other OECD country. That progress is now threatened by regressive measures such as cuts in child and family benefits (Miller and Hevey 2012). In an analysis of *Children of the Recession*, UNICEF (2014) argues that despite increasing inequality and disadvantage, it is by no means inevitable that children should be the most enduring victims of a financial crisis. Inequality lessens when the weight of the recession falls on more affluent households while poorer sectors of society are still protected by existing public policies and safety nets. If the impact is disproportionately felt by those on lower incomes then inequality is aggravated. UNICEF (2014) highlights how a number of countries successfully managed to limit, or even reduce, child poverty during the recession pointing out that impact on those at the bottom of the income scale is affected by existing economic structures, social safety nets and policy responses. In England, as welfare and public services continue to be cut in the name of austerity, the policy discourse about child poverty has shifted the explanation for poor outcomes onto inadequate parenting rather than lack of financial resources (Mathers et al. 2014; Simpson et al. 2015). The current policy agenda is firmly committed to a neoliberal perspective that disregards structural features and views family welfare as an individual responsibility and the result of personal enterprise. Policy priorities are concentrated on reducing the state's duty to support its citizens. This alters the obligation for responding to social problems, fragmenting provision so that business models and community action are now an accepted part of the education system. Ball (2013) argues that the more fuzzy and patchy the system is, the harder it becomes for those without the 'right' cultural assets to navigate. This makes perspectives of readiness as a deficit label particularly difficult for marginalised and disadvantaged families to resist.

Discussion points:

- How can schools and preschool settings work to promote social justice and address deep inequalities that can be obscured by a focus on school readiness?
- What is the role of high-quality early years education in 'narrowing the gap'? To what extent is readiness presented as a social panacea? What assumptions underpin policy initiatives that focus on readiness and what are their implications?

Policy: solution or problem?

Miller and Hevey (2012) suggest that the children's policy agenda might be considered too important to leave to politicians' whims and that a core programme for the long term should be agreed on a cross-party basis. They acknowledge the difficulty of achieving this however, given the contentious nature of policy-making and lack of appetite for taking a longer view. In reality a concern with quick results prevails and policy frameworks are mostly shaped by ideological beliefs and a concern to be re-elected.

In recent years neoliberalism – the 'irrational belief that the market can both solve all problems and serve as a model for structuring all social relations' (Giroux 2015: 170) – has become the globally dominant political discourse. This perspective privileges marketisation over citizenship and human rights, raising serious challenges for early years education (Sims and Waniganayake 2015). As Urban (2014) argues, defining a situation as 'economic' or 'financial' is likely to lead to economic questions and answers and prevents other views being taken into account. Neoliberal, market-driven policies are at odds with notions of ECEC as a public good and produce a system in which early years provision has become a commodity, driven by economic rather than educational interests. This distorts the readiness debate in a number of different ways. It positions ECEC as utilitarian preparation for schooling; demands are made for short-term measurable outcomes to demonstrate value for money and it creates conflict for parents who look to early entry to school as a relief from high childcare costs (Blake and Finch 2000). Sandel (2012) points out there are moral limits to markets complicating 'the distinction between . . . explaining the world and improving it' (p. 89).

These dilemmas caused the writers of the Cambridge Primary Review (CPR) to question whether policy is a solution or a problem (Alexander 2010). The Review voices concern about the process of policy, suggesting that wider problems of British democracy in retreat are mirrored in education. Issues identified include:

> the questionable evidence on which some key educational policies have been based; the disenfranchising of local voice; the rise of unelected and unaccountable groups taking key decisions behind closed doors; the "empty rituals" of consultation; the authoritarian mindset; and the use of myth and derision to underwrite exaggerated accounts of progress and discredit alternative views. (CPR 2010: 2)

These are all strategies that have been used in connection with early years provision and apply to the readiness debate. Consultation gives an impression of democracy but has little effect on how policy decisions are reached. Similarly research findings, even those commissioned by the government itself, are used or disregarded according to whether they support policy priorities. Evidence 'does not speak for itself' but lends itself to a range of alternative policy solutions (Miller and Hevey 2012: 171). Osgood (2006a) argues that 'dominant (government) discourses in teacher professionalism assert particular realities and priorities that are in stark polarity to those of practitioners' (p. 189). As a result, genuine frustration is felt by those with a significant role in young children's education at the way a standards agenda serves to endorse the whole apparatus of targets, testing, performance tables and inspection, distorting young children's schooling for questionable returns (CPR 2010). There is a feeling that policy guidelines and frameworks are being used as a means of legitimising initiatives claimed as being for a common good, but which can conflict with effective practice. The expectation that young children should be made ready for school is one of the most striking examples of this effect.

Discussion point:

- Mathers et al. (2014) identify a range of measures that should be met if the two-year-old offer is to be effective. What are the challenges of provision for very young children is schools? How can 'schoolification' of such provision be resisted?

Autonomy versus performativity

Increased investment in the early years sector has brought with it increased accountability and greater regulation of services and institutions. Normalising frameworks that regulate educational practice deploy a range of technologies to monitor and assess both the education system itself and the individuals within it.

These include standards, goals, performance tables, inspection, audits and guidelines. It is not only children's performance that is measured and monitored by government, but that of teachers and early years practitioners is also scrutinised and held to account. Regulation has moved beyond ensuring the entitlements of children and families are met and become instead top-down control and explicit prescription. This has implications for professionalism and autonomy, both of which are undermined by tightly defined outcomes that take little account of professional knowledge and expertise. Teachers' professional responsibility has been reframed as accountability, but when that accountability is to officialdom rather than to children themselves then tensions are inevitable.

Policy directives set out targets decided by politicians and policy-makers who have little knowledge of how young children learn and develop. Inspection criteria for determining quality are shaped by these same targets, creating stresses for early years teachers who are often torn between responding to children's own needs and interests or fulfilling government targets and outcomes. So quality standards and outcome-oriented practice can militate against pedagogical values and put at risk the very readiness they are intended to address. Expectations of a return on public investment mean that teachers are valued for what they produce rather than for what they do – 'good' teachers are those who produce good results and high levels of school readiness. Although official notions of readiness may be misconceived, as this book has argued, teachers are nonetheless assessed in terms of how well they meet these criteria. As a result of this 'regulatory gaze' (Osgood 2006b) many feel pressured to adopt the teacher-led instruction that is expected of them despite knowing this approach is likely to demotivate children and undermine their enthusiasm for learning.

It is a struggle to sustain quality in the face of externally imposed standards that limit flexibility and privilege ideology over professional knowledge and expertise. The language of 'curriculum delivery' reduces the teacher's role to that of a technician concerned with the transfer of knowledge and positions children as passive learners. Goouch (2008) suggests that many educators resort to 'strategic compliance' (p. 93) in the face of policy frameworks that construct teaching as a technical act. Regulation and control promotes technicist practice and a climate that encourages 'performativity' in pursuit of 'the best possible input/output equation' (Lyotard 1994: 43). This has had the effect of producing compliant educators who focus on how to meet requirements rather than critiquing the standards they are required to address (Sims and Waniganayake 2015).

Teaching is more than technical practice; it is a complex human activity that requires minute-by-minute decision-making in response to myriad changing circumstances. Professional autonomy is threatened by overly defined prescription. It denies the professional judgement required to adapt to constantly evolving contexts; in fact Davis (2013) questions whether such a thing as 'teaching methods' can really be said to exist at all. Early years practice that develops genuine readiness, rather than focusing on disembedded knowledge, is not amenable to the 'input/output equation[s]' Lyotard speaks of. The Tickell Review of the EYFS (2011) recognised the importance of autonomy and professional judgement stating that 'skilled teachers and practitioners should be attuned to each child's level of development, to their pace of learning, and to their abilities and interests – *and should determine the most effective approach to interacting with children to guide their development*' (p. 35, emphasis added).

Discussion point:

• What are the fundamental values that frame the readiness debate? How might the early childhood community build consensus on a rationale for early years education?

The importance of qualifications

Whether viewed from an educational perspective in terms of what best supports young children's learning, or from a more utilitarian standpoint of human capital discourse, well-qualified early years teachers are crucial. Findings from the EPPE Report (Sylva et al. 2004) were behind the development of graduate status for practitioners working with children from birth to five years and Ofsted ratings show strong correlation between higher qualifications and high-quality provision (Ofsted 2015). For this reason the Economist Intelligence Unit recommends funding should be prioritised towards human capital development ahead of infrastructure and technology (EIU 2012). Regardless of any difference in perspective on the readiness debate, all are agreed on the need for well-trained teachers. Yet the situation in regard to training opportunities for those wishing to specialise in teaching young children is far from clear and deprofessionalisation of staff, referred to above, poses threats for high-quality training.

Developmentally and pedagogically, early years is a distinctive stage requiring teachers to have in-depth child development knowledge and corresponding pedagogical skills. Recognising the wealth of evidence indicating the necessity of a responsive approach for effective teaching up to at least the end of Year 1, the Nutbrown Review (2012) recommended a specialist Early Years teaching qualification focusing strongly on pedagogy. Covering ages from birth up to seven years, it would include Key Stage 1 as well as the Early Years Foundation Stage. This proposal would ensure continuity in pedagogical approach and provide appropriate learning and teaching opportunities for young children despite the exceptionally early entry to school within the UK.

Nutbrown's recommendations have not been taken up. Currently a number of anomalies exist in relation to teachers for the youngest children and there is lack of clarity in references to *qualified teachers* and *early years teachers*. The differentiation is between those who have Qualified Teacher Status (QTS) and those without. Early Years Initial Teacher Training (EYITT) prepares graduates to work with children up to the age of five years but does not have the attached status necessary to be employed as qualified teachers in schools. Teachers deemed qualified (i.e. those with QTS) are less likely to have qualifications specifically focused on the holistic developmental needs of younger children. QTS training covers three to eleven years of age and focuses on academic learning. At the same time, disparity in pay and conditions renders EYTs 'second class' teachers (Eisenstadt et al. 2013: 2) so until equal status and career opportunities are available, early years teaching is likely to be a less attractive option for high-quality candidates.

An additional factor that presents challenges for those concerned with teacher education is the way official assumptions are embedded in professional standards and teacher training requirements (CPR 2010). Teachers' Standards set the agenda for teacher training and send strong messages about the core role of teachers of young children and the purpose of their work. Standards subsequently shape the educational experiences offered to young children – for example the narrow requirement to use systematic synthetic phonics affects how early literacy is taught and the range of strategies with which students become conversant. A major concern is the absence of play identified in the Teachers' Standards (Early Years) disregarding the crucial role of play in young children's learning and development (Evangelou et al. 2009). Instead, a standard requiring EYTs to demonstrate how they engage with the continuum of education through KS1 and KS2 suggests that the value of their work lies in how it leads to later schooling. The perspective promoted through professional standards inevitably affects what trainee teachers perceive to be the role expected of them and what they take care to demonstrate to assessors, teaching practice supervisors and headteachers. In this way there is a danger that the 'strategic compliance' identified by Goouch (2008) becomes part of teacher training. The Cambridge Primary Review laments that centrally-determined versions of teaching are all that many younger teachers know, even when research evidence shows these to be flawed (CPR 2010). Sims and Waniganayake (2015) share their concerns, asserting that 'we are increasingly educating students (even at higher degree levels) to accept the official discourse and to operate within that discourse' (p. 339).

Top-down control over the content and curriculum of teacher training courses means that programmes become a conduit for disseminating official policy objectives rather than enabling students to engage in deep level learning. Professional development has 'increasingly taken on a technical, competencies-and-skills connotation' (Oberhuemer 2005: 7) rather than being a transformative, educational process. In this context, reflection risks becoming narrowly focused on technical teaching strategies and evaluating implementation and there is less chance to engage in more critical reflection on fundamental values and pedagogical assumptions. In addition, the increase in school-based ITT reduces student teachers' opportunities for professional reflection and critical debate. The ability to articulate the values and principles underpinning how they work is an essential element of effective teaching and a strong preventative against technical practice. Requirements to achieve prescribed outcomes on the other hand are more likely to encourage a performative approach unable to see beyond evaluating practice against set targets: this has implications for how teachers understand readiness.

Discussion points:

- Research, independent reviews and official policy are all agreed on the importance of highly qualified early years practitioners. How do robust qualifications impact on the readiness debate? Development of a specialist early years training programme, carrying Qualified Teacher Status and having a strong focus on pedagogy has been recommended as the graduate qualification for those working with children up to and including age six (Nutbrown 2012; BERA/TACTYC 2014). With clear mechanisms for those with existing qualifications such as EYPS and Early Years Teacher to meet the criteria, what would be the benefits of this move? How would it impact on issues of readiness?
- What do you understand by 'professional knowledge'? Who decides what constitutes 'knowledge' and where does it derive from? How does knowledge relate to values and what is their connection to readiness? What is the relationship between professional standards and professional knowledge? To what extent might contradictions arise between these as a basis for practice?

Direct instruction versus play-based approaches

The contemporary audit culture focuses on learning and teaching as preparation for assessment so that an overwhelming emphasis on performance distorts teaching (Ball 2013). It is commonly recognised that 'teaching to the test' affects not only teachers' but also parents' approach to young children's learning (CPR 2010). This puts playful pedagogies at risk because their benefit may be less apparent and less amenable to measurement. The consequence of testing is that children learn to do tests but genuine learning that supports longer term academic success includes the ability to solve problems, to consider why things happen and to work with others to find solutions. These are not teachable processes: they require active, experiential learning providing opportunities for young children to process information in a way that makes personal sense. Bingham and Whitebread (2012: section 2.3) suggest that an explanation for the trend towards direct instruction may be found within the early years profession itself. They concede that some play programmes may have lacked thoughtful planning, implementation and assessment with a 'sit-back-and-watch' approach towards supporting child development infiltrating some provision. In such cases, when teaching methods fail to support satisfactory development, policy-makers blame play itself rather than understanding how play requires support from highly qualified, trained and skilled practitioners with a deep understanding of its role in children's learning (Moyles 2010; Sylva et al. 2010). Whilst it is understandable how such a conclusion might arise, a response that replaces poorly planned play provision with direct instruction does not address the problem.

The message of the EYFS might be regarded as rather ambiguous in relation to play. Goouch (2008) points out irony in the fact that, despite a key principle of play being something children choose to do so that they cannot be coerced into play, acknowledgement of it as a means of learning has made play 'statutory' within the EYFS. Identification of learning outcomes also sits uneasily alongside play as a natural learning strategy of young children. Moss (2014) suggests that by these means the EYFS provides an 'abstract map of how children are supposed to be at a given age' (p. 41). Such a universalising tendency reduces the likelihood that teachers can join in play activities without motives more related to curriculum objectives than children's own agendas and interests. Goouch (2008) criticises play used as 'invisible pedagogy' in this way so that it becomes 'a devious construct of teachers to secretly seduce children into pre-set learning agendas' (p. 99).

Because of pressure to achieve certain outcomes, teachers' control over learning by means of activities giving a superficial appearance of play are more likely to occur in school classrooms than preschool provision. Payler (2007) observed this difference in the learning opportunities experienced by four-year-old children in Reception class as opposed to a preschool playgroup. Although teachers working within the Early Years Foundation Stage curriculum in schools may believe they are enabling playful learning, this is not always the case. Inveigling children to follow pre-planned 'play' activities that hold little meaning for children themselves is counterproductive. Payler (2007) notes how tightly controlled adult agendas within the classroom reduce young children's agency and therefore their genuine involvement. As a result, she suggests 'doing school', rather than understanding the meaning behind their actions becomes of primary importance to children (p. 247). Play-based learning, where young children can exercise control and agency, is necessary for them to develop understanding through making connections and building on what they already know. Activities that attempt to transmit knowledge to children, rather than providing the environments, resources and, above all, interactions that enable them to construct it for themselves, cannot be regarded as play (Moyles 2010). Concerns about the very young age that children enter school prompt such attempts to present academic content in the guise of play, but this approach can never offer a solution to readiness. Vecchi (2004) warns that 'decontextualised objects and situations lead[s] to thinking in separate fragments and mistaking information for knowledge' (p. 19). She points out that knowledge can only be obtained by placing parts in relation to each other, a process undermined by a school culture that discriminates against children's approaches to exploration, understanding and construction of reality.

A curriculum-focused approach in place of playful learning and teaching also impacts on readiness by impairing young children's performance through stress or anxiety. Emphasis on literacy and numeracy comes at the expense of social and emotional development, opportunities to develop self-regulation abilities and positive learning dispositions. The strong connection between learning and socio-emotional development means a considerable portion of teachers' time and attention is taken up by dealing with behaviour issues (Aubrey and Ward 2013). Many young children will struggle to pay attention or follow instructions as they are significantly less mature than those starting school in most other countries and the academic demands made are greater. Classroom environments founded on play support the development of executive functions whereas control of outcomes by the teacher undermines children's sense of autonomy and motivation. Executive functions such as working memory and inhibitory control are likely to be over-whelmed by academic content too complex for children to be able to make their own meanings (Blair and Raver 2015) whereas open-ended play experiences enable children to make sense and consolidate their learning (see Chapters 2 and 3).

Discussion points:

• How can teachers support children's own lines of enquiry and resist the down-ward pressures of the National Curriculum?
• To what extent are young children 'universalised' by curricular frameworks? How do observations and assessment contribute to this process?

Final thoughts and further critical prompts

It is in the nature of modern education systems that schooling is extended rather than reduced. Although the school starting age in the UK is exceptionally early, cultural, economic and political reasons mean it is unlikely to be raised. Therefore debate should concentrate on the circumstances and nature of early educational provision. Downward pressure and demands that children be made 'school ready' have implications for all those involved in the Early Years Foundation Stage and first years of school, especially now when children as young as two years of age are entering provision located within schools. There is a need to think beyond the cur-rent dichotomy between 'ready children' and 'ready schools' to take a broader per-spective that embraces sociocultural, historical, economic and political dimensions.

Readiness is complex and contingent; it is constructed within the system dynam-ics between individuals, institutions and governance. A 'competent system' (Urban et al. 2011) depends on reciprocal relationships between all these layers, embrac-ing knowledge, practices and values. Consequently it must also take account of domains that frame knowledge, such as teacher training, professional development and research (including how this is funded, designed and the ideological paradigms within which it operates). There are no straightforward answers or solutions of the sort that policy-makers seek, but rethinking readiness can open up a more flexible and responsive appraisal of the issues. In the current climate it is often the case that 'audit culture triumphs over critical thinking' (Giroux 2015: 123) so re-evaluation may also help rebut some of the more damaging misconceptions about what it means to be ready for school. This section identifies further discussion points and reflective prompts to inform dialogue and debate and support critical examination of the issues.

• Can readiness for school be identified? Who is able to make such a judgement? What are the dangers of assessing readiness for school? What are the risks of not doing so?
• How do organisational issues – for example a single point entry system so that all young children begin in school in September – affect young children's

school experiences? To what extent are these arrangements for administrative convenience rather than children's benefit and well-being? How might some of the issues raised be overcome?

- Children's capabilities are not constant. Each has an individual and unique development trajectory and skills will vary depending on circumstances and context. What are the implications of this for assessment in the early stages of school? How does it affect fixed concepts of readiness?
- If children are accepted into school at a very early age, then they need provision that meets their needs. What measures can schools take to counteract 'the age effect' for summer-born children? How can teachers ensure assessments don't disadvantage less mature or less experienced children so that a label becomes a self-fulfilling prophecy?
- What are the implications of the early school starting age for children with disabilities and special needs? What would be the effect(s) of monitoring SEN referral rates in relation to birth date and age position in the class?
- Sociocultural factors do not operate independently but interact. Young children are intimately connected to their family and their community so factors in their environment evidently influence their learning and development. How can schools and preschool settings ensure their provision is meaningfully aligned to the concerns of their local communities?

Matters relating to these discussion points have been addressed both in this and in previous chapters. They are offered here to support critical scrutiny of issues surrounding school readiness and to stimulate debate.

Conclusion

Early childhood provision is founded on implicit constructions of childhood that have implications for what is regarded as readiness (Brooker 2008). Starting school is a point when these constructions may be in contention so tensions arise as different assumptions shape what is considered to be a 'good start' to education.

Current official publications suggest that the idea of school readiness is likely to continue to dominate government views of early years policy and provision. In a culture of accountability, of particular concern is the use of the concept to measure outcomes and assess the impact of investment. As the definition of what constitutes readiness is so difficult to determine, then it follows that assessing readiness must be even more so and a focus on children's performance is likely to result in a dangerous narrowing of the curriculum. Experience from the USA suggests that superficially simple measures of school readiness can be used in attempts to shape provision offered to young children and inappropriate assessment tools imposed on practitioners.

Young children's school start is an important life event that requires an interactive relationship between child, family, school, community and the wider environment. Official discourses of readiness construct young children (especially those from marginalised and vulnerable groups) as 'lacking' in relation to predetermined measures. This denies, or disregards, and potentially undermines the many competencies and strengths they bring with them to school. The ecological model of school readiness set out here provides a contextually relevant way to consider readiness as an element of a dynamic, ecological system. It acknowledges children's own agency and is sensitive to their environments, culture and communities. I contend that this offers a more helpful way of considering readiness, avoiding the entrenched positions of 'ready schools' versus 'ready children'.

Policy is a human technology, a mechanism intended to bring about certain social effects, but technological models of professional action see only one perspective (the search for 'what works') disregarding critical engagement with the issues. Working with young children is a democratic and moral endeavour (McDowall Clark and Murray 2012) and not a technical practice to bring forth standardised products in the service of the knowledge economy. The seemingly simple notion of readiness is too easily colonised for instrumental purposes, so early years teachers must be alert to limiting deficit discourses that attempt to shape all children to fit one predetermined mould. This is not an easy task but keeping in mind the purpose of early years education can help professionals resist political control of early years practices. As Ball (2013) makes clear '[n]either democracy, inclusion, nor equity, are end states, they are things that will always need to be struggled over' (p. 40). Examining the research evidence is fundamental to weighing arguments and making decisions, but it must also be remembered that evidence is not neutral; it can be used to bolster a variety of ideological positions. The intention of this book has been to open up and interrogate the topic of school readiness, to find a way through tangled arguments, contradictions and assumptions and encourage debate. Critical examination can contribute to providing optimal conditions for children's early educational encounters, regardless of the age that they begin school. It is hoped that greater understanding of background evidence and the issues at stake can empower teachers, early years practitioners, students and their tutors to reflect on ideas, enter into shared dialogue, be willing to ask critical questions, challenge dominant ways of thinking and when necessary resist inappropriate expectations and policy initiatives that go against the best interests of young children in their care.

References

Adams, S., Alexander, E., Drummond, M. and Moyles, J. (2004) *Inside the Foundation Stage: recreating the reception year: final report*, London: Association of Teachers and Lecturers.

Alexander, R. (2010) *Children, their world, their education, final report and recommendations of the Cambridge Primary Review*, London: Routledge.

Allen, G. (2011) *Early intervention: the next steps*. London: Cabinet Office.

Aubrey, C. and Ward, K. (2013) Early years practitioners' views on early personal, social and emotional development, *Emotional and Behavioural Difficulties*, Vol 18 (4): 435–447.

Ball, S. J. (2013) *Education, justice and democracy: the struggle over ignorance and opportunity*, Policy paper for the Centre for Labour and Social Studies, London: CLASS.

Bennett, J. (2013) A response from the co-author of 'a strong and equal partnership', in P. Moss (ed), *Early childhood and compulsory education: reconceptualising the relationship*, London: Sage.

BERA/TACTYC (2014) Early years: policy advice and future research agendas, available at http://tactyc.org.uk/wp-content/uploads/2013/11/Early-Years-Policy-BERA-TACTYC.pdf. Accessed June 25, 2016.

Bingham, S. and Whitebread, D. (2012) *School readiness: a critical review of perspectives and evidence*. Report prepared for TACTYC, available at www.tactyc.org/projects/. Accessed June 25, 2016.

Blair, C. and Raver, C. C. (2015) School readiness and self-regulation: a developmental psychobiological approach, *Annual Review of Psychology*, Vol 66: 711–731.

Blake, M. and Finch, S. (2000) *Survey of the movement of children from playgroups to reception classes*, London: National Centre for Social Research.

Bronfenbrenner, U. (1979) *The ecology of human development*, Cambridge, MA: Harvard University Press.

Brooker, L. (2005) Learning to be a child: cultural diversity and early years ideology, in N. Yelland (ed), *Critical issues in early childhood education*, Maidenhead: Open University Press.

Brooker, L. (2008) *Supporting transitions in the early years*, Maidenhead: Open University Press.

Cambridge Primary Review (CPR) (2010) *Cambridge Primary Review briefings: the final report*, available at www.primaryreview.org.uk. Accessed June 25, 2016.

Consortium of Institutions for Development and Research in Education in Europe (CIDREE) (2007) *The education of 4- to 8-year-olds: re-designing school entrance phase*, Brussels: CIDREE/DVO.

Dahlberg, G., Moss, P. and Pence, A. (2013) *Beyond quality in early childhood education and care: postmodern perspectives on the problem with quality* (3rd ed), London: Routledge.

Davis, A. (2013) To read or not to read: decoding synthetic phonics, *Impact: Philosophical Perspectives of Education Policy*, Vol 20: 1–38.

Department for Education (DfE) (2011) *Supporting families in the Foundation years*, London: DfE.

Department for Education (DfE) (2014) *Statutory framework for the Early Years Foundation Stage*, DFE-00337-2014, London: DfE.

Economist Intelligence Unit (EIU) (2012) *Starting well: benchmarking early education across the world*, London: Economist Intelligence Unit, available at www.economistinsights.com/leadership-talent-innovation/analysis/starting-well. Accessed June 25, 2016.

Eisenstadt, N. (2012) Poverty, social disadvantage and young children, in L. Miller and D. Hevey (eds), *Policy issues in the early years*, London: Sage.

Eisenstadt, N., Sylva, K., Mathers S. and Taggart B. (2013) *More great childcare: research evidence*, Oxford: University of Oxford and Institute of Education.

Evangelou, M., Sylva, K., Wild, M. and Glenny, G. (2009) *Early years learning and development: literature review*, London: DCSF.

Fabian, H. and Dunlop, A.-W. (eds) (2007) *Informing transitions in the early years: research, policy and practice*, London: OUP/McGraw Hill.

Field, F. (2010) *The Foundation Years: preventing poor children becoming poor adults. The report of the Independent Review on Poverty and Life Chances*. London: Cabinet Office.

Giroux, H. (2015) *Dangerous thinking in the age of the new authoritarianism*, Boulder, CO: Paradigm Publishers.

Goouch, K. (2008) Understanding playful pedagogies, play narratives and play spaces, *Early Years*, Vol 28 (1): 92–102.

Graue, E. (2006) The answer is readiness: now what is the question?, *Early Education and Development*, Vol 17 (1): 43–56.

Hirsh-Pasek, K., Golinkoff, R.M., Berk, L. and Singer, D. (2009) *A mandate for playful learning in preschool: presenting the evidence*, New York: Oxford University Press.

Lyotard, J.-F. (1994) *The postmodern condition: a report on knowledge*, Minneapolis, MN: University of Minneapolis Press.

Marmot, M. (2010) *Fair society, healthy lives: strategic review of health inequalities in England*, available at www.marmotreview.org.uk. Accessed June 25, 2016.

Mathers, S., Eisenstadt, N., Sylva, K., Soukakou, E. and Ereky-Stevens, K. (2014) *Sound Foundations. A review of the research evidence on quality of early childhood education and care for children under three: implications for policy and practice*, Oxford: University of Oxford and The Sutton Trust.

McClelland, M. and Wanless, S. (2015) Introduction to the special issue: self-regulation across different cultural contexts, *Early Education and Development*, Vol 26 (5–6): 609–614.

McDowall Clark, R. (2013) *Is there room for the child in partnership with parents?* Available at www.tactyc.org.uk/pdfs/Reflection-McDowall-Clark.pdf. Accessed June 25, 2016.

McDowall Clark, R. (2016) *Childhood in society for the early years* (3rd ed), London: Sage.

McDowall Clark, R. and Murray, J. (2012) *Reconceptualising leadership in the early years*, Maidenhead: Open University Press.

Miller, L. and Hevey, D. (eds) (2012) *Policy issues in the early years*, London: Sage.

Moss, P. (2014) *Transformative change and real utopias in early childhood education: a story of democracy, experimentation and potentiality*, London: Routledge.

Moyles, J. (ed) (2010) *Thinking about play: developing a reflective approach*, Maidenhead: Open University Press.

Murray, J. (2015) Early childhood pedagogies: spaces for young children to flourish, *Early Childhood Development and Care*, Vol 185 (11–12): 1715–1732.

National Children's Bureau (NCB) (2013) *Greater expectations: raising aspirations for our children*, London: NCB.

Nutbrown, C. (2012) Foundations for quality: the independent review of early education and childcare qualifications. Final report, available at www.gov.uk/government/publications/nutbrown-review-foundations-for-quality. Accessed June 25, 2016.

Oberhuemer, P. (2005) Conceptualising the early pedagogue: policy approaches and issues of professionalism, *European Early Childhood Education Research Journal*, Vol 13 (1): 5–16.

Ofsted (2014) *Are you ready? Good practice in school readiness*, available at www.ofsted.gov.uk/resources/140074. Accessed June 25, 2016.

Ofsted (2015) Inspection outcomes of early years providers by staff qualifications, available at www.gov.uk/government/publications/inspection-outcomes-of-early-years-providers-by-staff-qualifications--2. Accessed June 25, 2016.

Organisation for Economic Co-operation and Development (OECD) (2006) *Starting strong II: early childhood education and care*, Paris: OECD.

Organisation for Economic Co-operation and Development (OECD) (2011) *Doing better for families*, available at www.oecd.org/es/soc/doingbetterforfamilies.html. Accessed June 25, 2016.

Osgood, J. (2006a) Professionalism and performativity: the feminist challenge facing early years practitioners, *Early Years*, Vol 26 (2): 187–199.

Osgood, J. (2006b) Deconstructing professionalism in early childhood education: resisting the regulatory gaze, *Contemporary Issues in Early Childhood*, Vol 7 (1): 5–14.

Payler, J. (2007) Opening and closing interactive spaces: shaping four-year-old children's participation in two English settings, *Early Years*, Vol 27 (3): 237–254.

Peters, S. and Dunlop, A.-W. (2014) Editorial, *Early Years*, Vol 34 (4): 323–328.

Ritchie, S., Clifford, R., Malloy, W., Cobb, C. and Crawford, G. (2010) Ready or not? Schools readiness for young children, in S.L. Kagan and K. Tarrant (eds), *Transitions for young children: creating connections across early childhood systems*, Baltimore, MD: Paul H. Brookes Publishing Company.

Sameroff, A. (2009) *The transactional model of development: how children and contexts shape each other*, Washington: American Psychological Association.

Sandel, M. (2012) *What money can't buy: the moral limits of markets*, London: Allen Lane.

Sanders, D., White, G., Burge, B., Sharp, C., Eames, A., McCune, R. and Grayson, H. (2005) *A study of the transition from the Foundation Stage to Key Stage 1*, London: National Foundation for Educational Research.

Sharp, C (2002) *School starting age: European policy and recent research*, Paper presented at the Local Government Association Seminar 'When Should Our Children Start School?', LGA Conference Centre, London, November 1, Slough: NFER.

Shields, P. (2009) 'School doesn't feel as much of a partnership': parents' perceptions of their children's transition from nursery school to Reception class, *Early Years*, Vol 29 (3): 237–248.

Simpson, D., Lumsden, E. and McDowall Clark, R. (2015) Neoliberalism, global poverty policy and early childhood education and care: a critique of local uptake in England, *Early Years*, Vol 35 (1): 96–109.

Sims, M. and Waniganayake, M. (2015) The performance of compliance in early childhood: neoliberalism and nice ladies, *Global Studies of Childhood*, Vol. 5 (3): 333–345.

Siraj-Blatchford, I., Sylva, K., Muttock, S., Gilden, R. and Bell, D. (2002) *Researching effective pedagogy in the early years (REPEY)*, DfES Research Report 356, London: DfES/HMSO.

Sylva, K., Melhuish, E., Sammons, P., Siraj-Blatchford, I. and Taggart, B. (2004) *The Effective Provision of Pre-School Education (EPPE) project: final report*. London: Institute of Education.

Sylva, K., Melhuish, E., Sammons, P., Siraj-Blatchford, I. and Taggart, B. (2010) *Early childhood matters: evidence from the effective Pre-School and Primary Education Project*, London: Routledge.

TACTYC (2011) *The Early Years Foundation Stage through the daily experiences of children*, Occasional paper No. 1, available at www.tactyc.org.uk/occasional-paper1.pdf. Accessed June 25, 2016.

Taguma, M., Litjens, I. and Makowiecki, K. (2012) *Quality matters in early childhood education and care: United Kingdom (England)*, Paris: OECD.

Tickell, C. (2011) *The early years: foundations for life, health and learning*, available at www.educationengland.org.uk/documents/pdfs/2011-tickell-report-eyfs.pdf. Accessed June 25, 2016.

UNICEF (2012) *School readiness: a conceptual framework*, New York: United Nations Children's Fund.

UNICEF Innocenti Research Centre (2014) *Report card 12. Children of the Recession: The impact of the economic crisis on child well-being in rich countries*, Florence: UNICEF Innocenti Research Centre.

Urban, M. (2014) Learning from the margins: early childhood imaginaries, 'normal science' and the case for radical reconceptualisation of research and practice, in M. Bloch, B. Swadener and G. Cannella (eds), *Reconceptualising early childhood care and education: critical questions, diverse imaginaries and social activism*, New York: Peter Lang.

Urban, M., Vandenbroeck, M., Van Laere, K., Lazzari, A. and Peeters, J. (2011) *Competence requirements in early childhood education and care, final report*, London and Brussels: European Commission, Directorate General for Education and Culture.

Vecchi, V. (2004) The multiple fonts of knowledge, *Children in Europe*, Vol 4: 18–21.

Wall, S., Litjens, I. and Taguma, M. (2015) *Early childhood education and care pedagogy review: England*, OECD, available at www.oecd.org/unitedkingdom/early-childhood-education-and-care-pedagogy-review-england.pdf. Accessed June 25, 2016.

SUBJECT INDEX

AUTHOR INDEX